THE HEART OF HEALING

From Trauma to Health and Harmony

CHRISTINE HIBBARD, PhD

BALBOA.
PRESS

A DIVISION OF HAY HOUSE

Balboa Press books may be ordered through booksellers or by contacting:

Balboa Press
A Division of Hay House
1663 Liberty Drive
Bloomington, IN 47403
www.balboapress.com
1 (877) 407-4847

Because of the dynamic nature of the Internet, any web addresses or links contained in this book may have changed since publication and may no longer be valid. The views expressed in this work are solely those of the author and do not necessarily reflect the views of the publisher, and the publisher hereby disclaims any responsibility for them.

The author of this book does not dispense medical advice or prescribe the use of any technique as a form of treatment for physical, emotional, or medical problems without the advice of a physician, either directly or indirectly. The intent of the author is only to offer information of a general nature to help you in your quest for emotional and spiritual well-being. In the event you use any of the information in this book for yourself, which is your constitutional right, the author and the publisher assume no responsibility for your actions.

Any people depicted in stock imagery provided by Thinkstock are models, and such images are being used for illustrative purposes only. Certain stock imagery © Thinkstock.

Print information available on the last page.

ISBN: 978-1-5043-7000-4 (sc)
ISBN: 978-1-5043-7001-1 (hc)
ISBN: 978-1-5043-6999-2 (e)

Library of Congress Control Number: 2016919548

Balboa Press rev. date: 12/09/2016

Praise for the Heart of Healing

"On this pilgrimage of spirit and service, Chris Hibbard learns transformational lessons of acceptance, surrender, and love. And we, her fellow travelers, learn them along with her."

James S. Gordon, MD, author of *Unstuck*, and founder and executive director for the Center for Mind-Body Medicine

"Chris Hibbard has written a wise and tender account of her quest to understand, experience, and offer healing—a journey that has taken her across the globe. If you are on your own journey of spiritual growth and healing, you could not ask for a more experienced, compassionate, and loving guide and companion than Chris in this beautiful memoir."

Rev. Diane Berke, founder and spiritual director, One Spirit Interfaith Seminary

"*The Heart of Healing* is both wise and literate. I couldn't stop reading it! Through a set of powerful stories with profound insights, we meet real people and actual situations that leave us with unforgettable lessons about life, death, and meaning."

Mark Gerzon, president of Mediators Foundation and author of *The Reunited States of America: How We Can Bridge the Partisan Divide*

"Dr. Chris Hibbard, a skilled trauma therapist, invites us to read her compassionate stories from traumatized people of war zones. She includes her own personal journey in trauma recovery and artfully leads us toward meaningful insights about healing. Read this book and gently engage your own healing while you are generously supported by Chris's distinctive voice for transformational wisdom in our own lives and around the world."

Diane Poole Heller, PhD, author of *Crash Course*, trauma therapist and tTrainer, and creator of DARe

"In this remarkable book, Dr. Chris Hibbard has opened her heart and mind with deep spiritual insights that help us do the same. Her personal story is woven in and out with the stories of real people around the world who are dealing with the pain and suffering of war to bring healing. As she lives with her own pain and does her own healing, she helps those she works with as they bring light, love, and hope to people in war-torn parts of our world. Dr. Hibbard has written this book with such compassion and understanding that we, the readers, see that now there is hope for the world and that light always overcomes darkness. This book really needs to be read at this time."

Gladys McGarey, MD, author and founder of the Foundation for Living Medicine

"Chris Hibbard is a master storyteller. The stories she weaves in *The **Heart of Healing*** have the power to shock us, push and expand our boundaries, and ultimately, inspire us with the resilience of the human heart. She begins at her home, where a child struggles with a speech impediment, then takes us to regions devastated by war. Her mission is to help relieve trauma. At times she collapses in tears, but in the end, she's sustained by the love that transcends borders and regions. This is a journey you won't forget."

Sara Davidson, author of *Loose Change, The December Project*, and *JOAN: 40 Years of Life, Loss, and Friendship with Joan Didion*

"I cherish this book, ***The Heart of Healing***, not only for its compelling wisdom and inspiration, but also because I cherish its author, Dr. Christine Hibbard. I know Chris to be a person of depth, a person surrendered to compassion, a person engaged in her commitments. Chris is also a fun and joyous person. These qualities and values coalesce to inspire a foundation of gifts that flow abundantly throughout this wonderful work. This is a book of depth and impact, clearly reminding us all that, ultimately, it is the heart that reveals the healing energies and pathway for a life that works… and matters."

Dr. Roger Teel, Spiritual Director, Mile Hi Church, Author of *This Life is Joy; Discovering the Spiritual Laws to Live More Powerfully, Lovingly And Happily*

"Chris Hibbard's pilgrimage is like no other. If you allow yourself to accompany her, she will guide you from the most elegantly beautiful, beatific moments, and then, with similarly natural ease, confidently and naturally shepherd you down a rocky slope of unimaginable human suffering. All the while, she remains fiercely honest about the paths that are being cut into her own soul as she goes. And she will invite you to do the same. For this radically extreme tension – between heart-shredding anguish, and moments full to overflowing with immeasurable grace – is the most truthful representation of this experience we all share, this thing we call life. "

Wayne Muller, Founder, The Center for Living Sabbath, Bread for the Journey, Bestselling author of *Sabbath*, and *A Life of Being, Having and Doing Enough*

"This tender, compelling memoir of love without borders is a treasure of hope and healing. Prepare to laugh, cry, and open your heart to miracles."

Joan Borysenko, PhD, *New York Times* best-selling author of *Minding the Body, Mending the Mind*

"In this moving memoir, Chris Hibbard takes us on an inspiring journey toward gaining inner peace and profound lessons through courage to embrace healing and offer assistance to others in desperate places around the world. Read these amazing stories and gift yourself with her honest self-revelations for transformation."

Jack Canfield, coauthor of the *Chicken Soup for the Soul* series

"*The Heart of Healing* communicates the code of life-giving love, brilliance, wisdom, and the spirit of everlasting courage. Chris's heartfelt memoir is based on life and love enough to carry us through anything that life can offer. This book is everybody's best friend."

Barbara Marx Hubbard, author of *Conscious Evolution*, futurist, and founder of the Foundation for Conscious Evolution

Contents

Foreword

Joan Borysenko, PhD

It's true what they tell you. Nature is profligate in the wake of a fire. You never know what seeds lie dormant in the dark folds of the blackened earth, patiently waiting to make a run for the light.

When the worst wildfire in Colorado history swept through our Boulder mountain community in the late summer of 2010, my husband and I—plus our dogs Sophie and Milo—escaped the blaze and found safety in the home of our friends, Chris and David Hibbard. Chris reminded us that the seeds of the magnificent lodgepole pine trees on our property are able to germinate only after fire cracks them open.

Chris knows the truth of that up close and personal. She, like all of us, has been through her own fires. The stories of trauma and resilience, of death and resurrection that Chris shares in this tender and compelling memoir have been an important part of her own personal growth and evolution. The wisdom of her rich and varied experience continues to enrich the lives of her psychotherapy clients, family, and friends.

When Chris returned from a trip to Kosovo, where she was part of a healing team assembled by psychiatrist Jim Gordon, I watched her grapple with the aftermath of the genocide. Listening to her account of the journey, I marveled at how her heart could hold such painful images: children standing around a mass grave in their schoolyard where the bodies of their murdered parents had been dumped, bombed-out buildings, and streets booby trapped with land mines.

People who work with those who have been wounded emotionally and physically often develop a condition called compassion fatigue. Another term for it is secondary trauma. The healer's own nervous system falls prey to the trauma of others as if it were his or her own. The result is depression and burnout.

Time and the comfort of family and friends helped heal Chris's wounds and prevent compassion fatigue from setting in. So did her remarkable ability to make meaning out of the devastation she witnessed in Kosovo and in the many other places around the world where she has shown up to help.

The process of finding meaning in suffering is key to resilience and stress hardiness. It is a spiritually based skill that comes naturally to Chris—a skill that is indispensable to the work that needs to be done by each one of us in these troubled times.

Psychiatrist and Holocaust survivor Viktor Frankl expressed this universal spiritual perspective powerfully in his classic book, *Man's Search for Meaning*. Love is the end and the means, the alpha and the omega of the human journey. Love is the hidden source from which all life flows in both its infinite joys and its unspeakable sorrows. This understanding is the transcendent loom on which all of Chris's touching stories are woven.

Chaos and destruction are the dark angels of evolution—at least potentially. The healer's role is to listen lovingly to the wounded, help them grieve what has been lost, and water the seeds of hope for what can be. This is the heart of healing that Chris describes so gracefully in this beautiful memoir of love without borders.

We are in a time in world history of global breakdown and renewal. Old systems are dying, and new ones are being born. It's a messy and often scary time. Fires of all sorts—literal and metaphorical—are breaking out worldwide. The message of Chris Hibbard's memoir—and the process of walking with her through the flames—is one of love and hope. Together we can and will bring a new world into being.

That is Chris's powerful message for our time.

Introduction

We Are All Connected through the Heart

In 1982 I was sitting in our outdoor hot tub in Boulder, Colorado, with my husband, David, our five-year-old son, Ryan, and our ten-year old daughter, Devin. We were playing a game where I would ask everyone in the tub, "If you had three wishes, what would you wish for?" All I wanted was a good night's sleep. But when it was Ryan's turn, he surprised us. We were sure he wanted a brand new bike, but instead he said, "I wish I could fly!" He splashed his small arms across the water. "And my second wish is that I want to be able to change sizes—from small to big." He cupped his little hands, then extended his arms as far as they could go. "My third wish is that I want to be invisible."

We were silent, and then I asked him, "Ryan, why would you want those three wishes?"

He firmly replied, "So that I can fly all around the world, and I can land on people's shoulders, and I can whisper in their ear, 'You're not alone.'"

Spiritual wisdom out of the mouth of babes. That's exactly what I wanted as a psychotherapist: to tell my clients that they were not alone during their challenges. "Flying all around the world" to do it did not come until a few years later, when I began to study different ways of healing in diverse cultures.

I do believe that we are never alone. A divine Source in the universe is guiding us, and people have many names for this Love that is always present. My own spiritual journey began in my heart—not in the spiritual textbooks that I read in my twenties. Ryan's words touched me deeply, because they were clearly a spiritual truth told straight from his young heart. This memoir comes straight from my heart.

At the end of the day, most people in this beautiful yet ever-changing and troubled world want to know if they have made a difference and contributed to the lives of others. No matter how small or large the act, we want our lives to be meaningful. I wrote this book because over the years I had extraordinary opportunities to witness aspects of healing at home and around the world that I never could have imagined. At this particular moment in history, I believe that we each have an opportunity to expand who we think we are and open to the possibility of global self-expression and service to humanity in a whole new way.

Colleagues and friends encouraged me to write about stories and experiences that have taught me valuable lessons. Part memoir and part healing journey, my writing is about diverse cultural approaches to healing. These approaches come from the work I've been privileged to participate in, starting with my own family, personal healing of my own, and teaching health care workers to reduce their emotional trauma and symptoms of PTSD (post-traumatic stress disorder) in postwar zones. I also have stories from the work that my husband, David, and I continue to do together at a hospital in Uganda, a nonprofit project that we cofounded in 2006.

David and I are both faculty members at the University of Colorado Medical School, Global Health Department. Our medical students spend six weeks at our Ugandan hospital. The challenging experience of serving in an understaffed and underequipped hospital, observing how limited and modern medicine complement one another, transforms how these students will practice medicine and be with patients in the future.

As a child, I grew up with a deep sense of the value of service, mainly from watching and listening to my mother. She taught her children that it isn't enough be happy in life. It was our responsibility to give back to others through service. At the ripe and wise age of ninety-nine, Mom was still serving in any way she could. She was quite a sight as she held onto her walker and gave pep talks to the homeless at my sister's volunteer project in Denver. The homeless folks loved her, and she loved them. Everyone's lives were enriched through the simple gift of human kindness.

Healing and service, and the way they bring people of disparate beliefs and cultures together in the heart, were the inspiration for writing these stories. I offer this volume to you, enriched by the precious gifts of love, healing, and the basic goodness of humanity I've received.

From the mid-1970s to the present, I've traveled around the world and witnessed a transformation of consciousness. Sometimes this transformation has been the result of extreme violence inflicted upon cultures, or very poor people helping each other in community, or others demonstrating a unity between people and the environment. People are waking up and discovering that we can work together and learn from each other in spite of differing points of view, that we can go beyond the boundaries that have limited us in the past.

We are also beginning to wake up to a new way of relating to each other and ourselves. Our childhood conditioning presents a false sense of identity, covering up the authenticity and goodness that is our true nature. Through my inner and outer work with what it means to be truly human, I began to feel what I call being truly whole, able to feel peace of mind not only when life is going well, but also in the midst of challenge. Many of these insights came when I took a risk, when I was forced to deal with a medical challenge, or when I was really scared. In those moments, my life sometimes took a turn for the better.

We now have wisdom available from cultures, religions, and the collective consciousness around the world that we did not have before the Internet. Expanding our worldviews and working with all of humanity is truly needed to heal all beings.

So how do we fully appreciate the value of life? I believe we are guided through life by a loving energy in the universe that we call God or the divine Source or any of a myriad of other names. We all experience fear, suffering, joy, and marvelous blessings along the way.

When I found myself called to work overseas in the postwar zone of Kosovo, one of my dearest friends cautioned me about going to such a dangerous place. She was going to Bali to guide a retreat on mind-body medicine, leaving on the same day I was to leave for Kosovo. She suggested I go with her as a companion on the trip. *Hmmm,* I wondered. *Going to the paradise of Bali or going to a war zone?* But a flame was being ignited in my heart, and I knew I had to listen to my heart's calling.

My memoir begins with a profound healing experience I received through my daughter. All healing begins at home. I also share some personal inspirational stories, including a near-death experience while river rafting, and my father's passing, which further shaped me and challenged me with my career and personal growth.

In the middle part of this book, I share experiences I had exploring different cultural paths to healing in New Zealand and Hawaii. One was working with refugees in Kosovo, because it was a pivotal period in my life. I felt blessed and privileged to work with people who had suffered so much from war.

In the last part of the book, I share stories about the challenges of growing older and the awareness and consciousness that promotes healing with less suffering. Other stories are about fieldwork in Syria, Uganda, and with Israeli/Palestinian women.

World events are challenging us today to develop a mature consciousness. Every opportunity we have to learn from our own personal challenges with healing increases our ability to move in the world for the benefit of all.

One warm, star-filled summer night when I was perhaps three years old, my father took me outside into the backyard and sat down on our swing with me in his lap. "Look up, Chris," he said, and my eyes widened as they took in the entire Milky Way. I remember feeling awe and wonder. Safe in my father's strong arms, I looked at the twinkling magic of the lights, and a love of the vast and mysterious universe took root within my heart.

Years later, as a biologist and psychotherapist feeling drawn to teach others about the mysteries of this vast universe and the nature of being human within it, I recognized the seeds of my calling to work around the world in that incandescent memory.

I have changed the names of the people I have worked with personally. I hope this memoir told from my own experience will enhance your dreams for love and healing permeating all of humanity. We can reach within ourselves inspired by stories of others' healing experiences and find love, faith, and surrender.

Chapter 1

A Daughter Teaches Acceptance

Accepting circumstances leads to healing.

"I—I—I w—want t—t—to g—go!" three-year-old Shannon struggled to say.

"You want to go where, Shannon?" I asked. She had tears in her eyes as she frowned and was silent. It was heartbreaking to see her sadness, confusion, and pain each time she tried to speak and failed. She would mouth the words, start to stutter, and then give up.

Toddlers often go through vocal cord adjustments, but I noticed something disturbing about Shannon's behavior. She was embarrassed and self-conscious. Most children her age don't notice when they stutter a little.

A week later, she strained at words most of the time and became really quiet. For the first time in over a year, Shannon didn't sing or talk at all. I wondered, *Is she picking up on all our stress over our growing medical center, growing family, and doctoral work?*

I was working on my PhD in clinical psychology. Shannon was almost three, the youngest of our three children. I found myself easily stressed in those days of juggling clinical work, doctoral work, and home life. Shannon was growing by leaps and bounds as she attended Montessori preschool, ballet class, and a toddler gymnastics class. She had been very independent and had spoken in long sentences nonstop.

I remember her with three children in her playgroup, confidently playing the role of the teacher. "Who wants to learn how to make apple pie today?" she asked them. Everyone's hands went up. "Then here is how we will do it." As I walked over to their play kitchen, Shannon exclaimed, "Mommy, I am the teacher today, and I will be a teacher when I grow up, too. I am going to teach all the children in the world!"

Later, when we realized Shannon might be developing speech issues, our first course of action was to take her to the University of Colorado's speech department for testing. I didn't want her to identify with a diagnosis, but David and I were desperate for help. As we entered the speech therapist's office, images of Shannon's once happy and lively spirit entered my mind, but now I saw anxiety on her face. She gave me a puzzled glance as the therapist asked her if she liked to play with dolls. Shannon gave a wary smile and held out her favorite doll.

The therapist told her he was going to take her into another room and ask her some questions. Her eyes were riveted on mine as he led her into the room. After testing, the chairperson of the department told us his assessment. He said with certainty, "Shannon has ten out of ten signs of being a stutterer for life. I suggest that she immediately start five sessions per week with a speech therapist to learn how not to stutter."

When we returned home, David wanted to start the speech therapy right away. I wanted some time to process the shocking news and get more information on the whole phenomenon. I asked, "What does this mean for Shannon's social and learning development, and most importantly, how will she feel about it all? How can we manage her needs with the huge amount of work and stress happening in our lives?" *And*, I thought, *when would we all be happily laughing again together?* Laughter was a key stress-management tool for our family.

As I walked our nearby hiking trail the next day, I reviewed my own emotional process. Being a stutterer for life certainly was not a life-threatening illness. Yet the image of Shannon embarrassed in front of her peers throughout school and struggling to learn gave me tremendous anxiety. She was already showing extreme signs of embarrassment. Remembering my own childhood self-consciousness when others made fun of me for ordinary behaviors, I felt sad about Shannon and what might lie ahead.

Our other two children were happily engaged in their lives and were excellent students. Academic studies came easily and naturally for them, so I felt afraid for Shannon. At the same time, I was determined not to transfer my fears onto her. I knew how powerful the effects of childhood trauma could be.

The next day, I dropped in on Shannon's preschool class to ask if her teachers were aware of her stuttering. The answer was "Yes, we are aware. She withdraws from others as she struggles for words." After discussing the situation with my main doctoral professor and supervisor, Dr. Bob Shaw, we decided that I should keep her out of the medical model and explore alternatives.

David wanted her to have some speech therapy, so we came to a compromise: one day each week a speech therapist would come over to the house and do exercises with Shannon under the guise of babysitting. Bob's idea was to let Shannon be our model: all of us closest to her were to stutter with her. If we stuttered with her, rather than trying to change her, we hoped she would feel less stressed and would outgrow her self-consciousness about stuttering.

David and I and our nanny, Bernice, who had been babysitting during my work hours the past two years, agreed to mirror Shannon's stuttering. Our other children, Devin and Ryan, agreed too, as did her teachers. Everyone involved let it occur as naturally as possible.

At first, Shannon looked at us curiously when we stuttered a little bit. Did she suspect what we were doing? One day, she finally struggled with the words needed to ask about her speech difficulties. With her face red and lips pinched, she painfully said, "M—m—mommy, w—w—why is it h—h—hard?"

Trying to keep my tears at bay, I reassured her by stuttering back, "S—sweetheart, h—h—how you talk is just fine with me. It will b—b—become much easier."

Shannon's situation was extremely painful for me. My anxiety level skyrocketed, knowing that David and I had to be especially calm for Shannon in spite of all the stress happening at our medical center.

Rolfing bodywork was suggested to loosen up Shannon's vocal chords, so I set up some sessions right away with a pediatric rolfer. She said she would be very gentle with Shannon. Seven-year-old Ryan agreed to go to some sessions as well, just so Shannon would go. We explained to Shannon before each session that it was good for both of them to have this work. Shannon managed to last for several twenty-minute sessions.

At night, when she was asleep, I would sit next to her crib, getting as close to her as possible and matching her breathing. I would whisper positive words of love to her, believing they would go to her subconscious. I repeatedly whispered, "I love you, Shannon, just the way you are," "The way you speak is fine with me," and "You are a beautiful and smart little girl." I did this every night for two months.

I held her and told her these words of love during the day when she was awake, and she looked at me intensely with those deep blue eyes and said, "N—n—no" and ran away. It was as if she thought I was lying. I wondered, *Am I lying to her and myself? Can I accept the way she is?*

In addition to my prayer work, I started to meditate every day. In my contemplation, I attempted to believe that Shannon would be okay being a stutterer for life. But my gut feeling was telling me that I wasn't there yet. Every day, I wondered how long it would take for me to absolutely accept her situation, however it turned out. *Who is suffering, me or my daughter?* I asked myself. It seemed to be me.

Meanwhile, while everyone else was getting used to joining Shannon's model, I was spending time each day allowing my sad feelings to surface and then trying to believe in the model working. *Why can't I just trust in God's great love and the process we've all started?* I thought. I had a hard time quieting my anxiety. I felt that

Shannon was indirectly telling me that if I could be okay with the way she was, she would be okay with it. *How can I let go of my fear and at the same time move forward with the appropriate healing steps for her condition?*

One warm and sunny fall day about two months into this whole process, Shannon and I were at the downtown outdoor mall. She was climbing on smooth rocks with a few other kids and sliding down the sides. I was stuttering a bit, along with the very few words that Shannon would stutter. A little boy called over to his mother, "Mom, this girl and her mommy talk funny!" Then he started to laugh.

I laughed out loud and held my breath to see how Shannon would respond. For the first time since her stuttering had started, she laughed too, with the little boy. *Is she finally accepting her possible fate? Am I?* In that moment, I felt the struggle begin to leave my body.

That night, after the whispered affirmation, I slept soundly for the first time in weeks and had a wonderful dream. Shannon and I were outside in the backyard near the flower garden. I saw all types of little angels dancing around and playing with her. I stood there in wonder, appreciating Shannon for the amazing little being that she was. I woke up smiling, feeling relaxed and happy.

That morning, when she stuttered and guardedly looked at me for a response, I told her once again that however she talked was fine with me. That's when she looked at me differently. I could see her little body relax and her breathing begin to steady. I noticed that my gut did not ache as usual. For the first time, I knew in my heart that if Shannon did become a stutterer for life, she would be okay. I would meet the challenge without all the anxiety and fear that I had associated with it.

The next day, I got a call from Shannon's preschool teacher, asking if the stress of our medical building and my doctoral work was over. "I wish," I sighed, "but not for three more months. Why do you ask?"

She replied, "Because Shannon has not stuttered once today, and she is talking a blue streak, just like before."

Shannon never stuttered again. Her giggling and nonstop talking returned. The chairman of the university's speech department was surprised, as Shannon was speaking clearly and confidently without therapy.

Shannon went on to become an eloquent speaker throughout her school years and graduated from Georgetown University with a master's degree. She has always spoken out clearly for those who can't find a voice for themselves. At age twenty-five, she was teaching first response at natural-disaster trainings all over the country and internationally. She has worked the last few years with scientists in other countries, including Egypt, Uzbekistan, Tajikistan, and Ukraine, and she is currently being recruited by the State Department to work overseas with US embassies.

I learned many things about healing during this experience. One that stands out the most is that our children want to be accepted by us as they are. My determination to accept Shannon unconditionally allowed me to surrender to the outcome. This not only strengthened my bond with her, it also allowed me to reprogram my insecurities and fears. My love for her became deeper in a way that any mother can know and understand.

In challenging times, it became easier to do my best to trust in life's process. Shannon grew up marching to the beat of her own drum. Knowing the importance of first accepting any circumstance that may come along and then doing what it takes to resolve it became a foundation for all my challenging times.

Chapter 2

Being Thrown into Fear

*Surrendering to fear and struggle while
trusting Spirit allows for healing.*

"This is so incredibly beautiful," I said joyfully, pulling my oar in rhythm with the other five friends on our raft. I felt pretty safe with our leader, Otsie, knowing that we would soon be riding a mean part of whitewater, called Skull, on the Colorado River.

"Yes!" exclaimed David. "Imagine three full days of natural beauty on the river looking at these gorgeous canyon walls!"

The sun sparkling on the crystal-blue water took my breath away. We could smell the pine trees as we drifted, enjoying the languid headwaters of the river. *I love the peace I feel on this river,* I mused.

Suddenly the river sped up, and we could see whitewater ahead. The raft was hit sideways by a rogue wave and then spun out from under me. I was stunned, but I scrambled into the float position we had been taught, my legs pointing downstream. It was hot, and the cool water felt good, so I wasn't too worried. Since I was wearing a life jacket, I didn't try to get back in the boat immediately. I had no idea that my relaxed attitude was going to get me in trouble.

The next moment, we hit the start of dangerous and continually thundering whitewater. "Get in the boat!" yelled David.

But the raft was moving at lightning speed. David jumped in to rescue me.

Otsie screamed, "Get back in the raft, David. Now!"

Registering the gravity of the situation, Oliver did not want two people in the water. They pulled David onto the raft. Seconds later, the raft shot ahead of me and was out of sight around a bend in the narrow canyon. For the next mile, I was alone and fighting to keep from drowning in the whirlpools of raging water that repeatedly sucked me under the surface.

Terrified, I tried to think what to do next. I remembered a story I had told about surrendering to the flow of the river. Apparently, I was at odds with the river's flow that day because I continued to be thrown into the gauntlet of rocks, whirlpools, and sinkholes. I started praying very hard. Exhausted, I knew I did not have the strength in my arms to push myself up from underneath the churning torrents of water one more time.

At that moment, I realized I might die. A still small voice inside me said it would be okay to die and become a part of the river. I experienced surrender. The altered state of acceptance gave me peace and relief from not having to struggle anymore.

Suddenly I realized I'd stopped moving. I was aware of the hot sun on my freezing skin and a solid rock beneath me. I was lying on a huge boulder, looking over a falls area, a big drop-off where the river cascaded through a chute between two huge boulders. The sound of the water was deafening.

Looking up, all I saw was high, sheer sandstone canyon walls and blue sky.

I thought, *How did I manage to get myself up onto this enormous rock when I am totally exhausted?* I had no idea. *Could divine grace have helped me onto the rock?* I was stunned at that thought. *The river held me in a way for me to live.*

I sat for what felt like hours on top of the huge rock, the sun beating down on me, and I thought, *Now I will surely die of heat exhaustion.* Nobody was coming down the river, and I couldn't see or hear any rescue helicopters overhead. I thought of my children and David and the fact that I had almost died in the river. I could not imagine not sharing the kids' lives with them as they grew into adulthood.

Around the bend upriver came three kayakers. They pulled over in an eddy and were strategizing the best route over the falls called Skull. I waved and hollered. "Can you help me?"

One by one they came near me, safely rolling over the falls. The last kayaker spotted me as he turned around to head downriver and yelled, "Nobody will be able to rescue you!"

I was stunned. *Now what?*

Just then, I spotted a raft coming downstream, holding six strong-looking men and a woman at the oars on the frame in the middle. She also pulled over at the eddy across the river to review her route over the falls. I screamed, "Help me!" as loud as I could, over the noise of the falls, making hand motions of "Can you pick me up?"

The women gave me a thumbs-up, and each man shook his head in disbelief.

They're thinking it's too risky, I thought.

The women then hand signaled me to be ready to jump onboard as her boat crested the falls. Adrenaline flooded my body. *I will have to be fast and will have only one shot.*

It seemed to happen in slow motion and also in an instant. One moment I was in the air; the next I had landed in the raft. The woman showed herself to be very strong as she yanked me into the raft with one hand while maneuvering the boat over the roaring falls with her other hand. Her raft landed perfectly: we were all very wet, but safe. I just lay on the floor of the raft all curled up, saying over and over, "Thank you, thank you. You are my river angel."

We rounded a bend in the river, and I heard her say, "There are your people over on the left bank, waiting for you." I sat up feeling very spacey and dizzy, most likely from dehydration and shock. My rafting friends cheered, helped me onto their raft, gave me a jacket for warmth, and thanked the women and men for picking me up.

"But where is David?" I asked.

"He climbed up the canyon wall to go look for you," said Otsie.

While waiting for David to return, some of my friends gave me grapes and water for rehydration while others held me to help with shock. David returned, and we were both overjoyed to see that the other was safe. We all waved goodbye to the people in the rescue boat.

Our group went on to spend two more days on the river, with me taking it very easy. I made sure to stay *in* the raft. At the end of the trip, we inquired at the permit station about the rescue boat. They told us no other boat was on the river that day that they knew of. *What?* I thought. *That doesn't make sense, but neither did my time in the river.*

Lessons keep on coming on a regular basis. Learning unconditional trust and its distinction from conditional trust is a big one. When I was in the river and knew I could no longer keep my head above water, in letting go I experienced an unconditional trust that I didn't understand at the time. It was an unspoken, implicit trust that what is optimal will happen.

This trust was different from what I had known before the rafting incident. The conditioned trust I had based my life on was dependent on the reliability of people and situations. Painful experiences and personal betrayals had disrupted unconditional trust; it was always subject to change. When I was a child, when my father said he would be at one of my school functions and did not show up, I was sad and disappointed. From then on, I relied on conditional trust.

The unconditional trust that I experienced that day in the river was different. It was not a trust in something, some person, or some situation; therefore, it was not diminished by circumstances. Now, with that trust experience behind me, I can more easily be with life's circumstances. I feel in my bones that I don't have to be so afraid if disastrous events happen. That fall into the river changed my life because it gave me an inherent trust in Spirit.

Many things happened over the coming months. I was processing my emotions more easily as they came up, much like riding the whitewater in the river. Instead of fighting and repressing them, I got better at letting my emotions wash over me and then letting them go. I also started working with people in the midst of the dying process and took a hospice volunteer training course. This led to developing a medical directive guide that David and I eventually published.

Almost dying that day gave me a new appreciation for the sacredness of the world every day. A feeling of overwhelming gratitude washes over me when I stay in the present moment, noticing the beautiful color of the trees and flowers in a new way. Through meditation, prayer, and contemplative experiences, I feel more connected to the Divine.

I will forever feel blessed by that river experience as I remember to embrace my fears and challenges. These lessons come more quickly as my soul pushes me into new growth. The world is moving so rapidly that sometimes I have a hard time catching my breath. Familiar water suddenly seems perilous with uncharted obstacles that shift with the changing river bottom. I hope this world and all of us in it can learn to swim with courage and divine grace in the amazing flow of the twenty-first century.

Chapter 3

A Father, Dying

Healing is about keeping our hearts and minds
open to dying into the unknown.

The hospital room was dreary and dark, and I was startled to see how frail and ill my father looked. His bed was only a few feet from the door with all the noise from bustling carts and loud voices. I closed the door and sat down on the side of his bed. Dad opened his steel-blue eyes and smiled. His skin was pale, his thinning hair messy, his face unshaven, and his skin markedly pale. And he had tubes attached to both bruised arms.

"Get me out of here, Chris," he pleaded with me.

"I will do everything I can, but I just arrived from Colorado. I need to go see Mom first," I softly replied, holding his thin, bruised hand. I felt so bad for him and said a silent prayer. "Are you breathing any better, Dad?" I asked.

"Not any better than when I was at home using my oxygen," he replied softly.

"Dad, I want to ask you to do something for me too. Would you answer some questions about how you want to die?" I had tears in my eyes. "It would really help all of us to know what you want."

"I don't want to talk about it," he said with fear in his eyes.

Why, I wondered, *do so many people in our society have such fear over death?* I felt sad that so many of us are too afraid to even talk about it.

Dad pushed the buzzer to call the nurse. He said angrily, "I have pushed this buzzer over and over to get the nurse and doctor here, and the nurse says he will come, but he never does!"

My father had always felt uncomfortable discussing death in general, let alone discussing his own dying process. I had always thought that his unfailing sense of humor had kept him alive over the past ten years. He was diagnosed with emphysema at age sixty. This scared him enough to cut back on smoking, but not enough to quit completely until years later.

I thought that his fear of death caused him to be more anxious. Perhaps the more he feared death, the more he feared life, and the less he truly lived. My work and training showed me that coming to terms with death helps open us to Spirit and healing. I had learned that we have to die to the ego in order to awaken to Spirit.

Leaving my dad at the hospital that cold winter day to drive to my childhood home, I wondered how I could help him to understand that he was dying and that hospice care would help all of us and would allow him to die with dignity at home.

When I arrived, my mother was worn out. She was reluctant to talk about Dad's dying process. Family members that lived nearby thought I was doing harm by bringing it up, and some begged me not to. We set up some home care for him, and I began the process of getting his affairs in order.

There was no doubt in my mind that he was dying. It was clearly written on his face. I had spent the last decade helping patients at our medical center with death and dying, counseling them on their deathbed. Dad's family practice doctor wouldn't talk to him about it, even though he told me Dad's death was imminent. When do we tell people that they can or need to let go and move on toward death?

Dad was released from the hospital the next day. That week I cooked and served him all his meals, massaged his legs, adjusted his oxygen and pillows, and did whatever he asked. I cooked Thanksgiving dinner for Mom and my brothers' families. What seemed most important to Dad was our being with him. His fear seemed to begin to dissipate, and he smiled more often.

In previous years, I had tried to engage Dad in a conversation about his mortality. It was always too uncomfortable for him, so I did not pursue it. I would rationalize the delay by saying, "Well, he is only seventy years old." But now I realized how important it is to have these discussions with our parents when they are well.

One afternoon that week, I approached Dad with some reflective questions about his life, and he agreed to my recording his answers.

"What do you feel was the greatest contribution you made over your lifetime?" I asked.

"Well, I would have to say it was raising you kids, and the work I did in the landscaping department at the college."

"Wait, I asked what your greatest contribution was, not your downfall!" I joked, referring to us kids. Humor always put him at ease.

I moved on quickly to address his wishes for his own memorial service before he became too tired. He seemed okay with it for the first time. I was deeply touched by his responses to all my questions and will always remember this special gift of sharing and tenderness. There was an intimacy I had not known with my father.

"Dad, what are you afraid of the most right now?" I asked.

"I'm afraid of going to the hospital again, afraid of suffering more pain, and afraid to appear before God and show Him my life," he confessed.

Wow, it is this great encounter that frightens him. Everything else seemed to vanish for him except that moment of judgment.

He added, "I know I haven't been as kind to others as I would have liked."

Back in Colorado, I had time to think and reflect. Workdays revolved around my children, David, and patient sessions. Hospice care was set up for Dad, which especially helped Mom. I felt blessed to have shared those sacred moments with my father. I had never felt so close to him. I tried to think of any unresolved issues I may have. We had resolved many over the years. I wondered, *How will I feel when he is gone?* And I realized that I would have to grow into the answer slowly and gently.

My father died at home with many loved ones around him. During his last days, I saw strength in my sister that I had not known before. Sharing this experience with her and my brothers brought us all closer. Dad died emotionally healthier than I had ever known him to be. He had made amends with one of my mother's sisters after many years of being angry toward her.

After Dad's death, my relationship with him moved into the realm of memory, and the way in which I had been his daughter was determined forever. At his memorial service, I let the truth of his passing move deeply into my heart. I recognized that I had become a different person, a person without a father, a person alone in a new way.

In the weeks that followed, I was sad and exhausted but also newly aware of and grateful for my family. I spent a lot of time by myself, making a conscious effort to grieve. I realized that by letting go, I did not lose him.

My father's dying process became a profound spiritual teaching for me. Christ and many spiritual masters hold that only in surrendering to death is real life found. Yet it is in ordinary events and death that we touch the mystery of life.

A few months later, I watched seven Tibetan monks constructing a beautiful, large sand mandala over a period of three days near our public library. They were demonstrating the notion of the impermanence of material life. Different geometric designs were created from sand in a ritual.

Each day I watched for half an hour as they made a circular geometric design out of different colors of sand by pouring it into an intricate pattern. The colors were a beautiful turquoise, orange, and light green. The monks were focused and peaceful as they worked.

At the end of the third day, they finished. I sat on a nearby bench and watched as they prayed aloud in Tibetan. They then very peacefully dismantled the beautiful mandala and swept it away.

For me, the sand symbolized Dad's physical existence and all of life, which was beautiful, doesn't last long, and is a blessing and a mystery. Yet the energy of our spirit lives on, and I surrendered again to this important lesson.

Chapter 4

Behind the Silence

Expressing yourself fully and trusting your intuition allows for healing.

Thirteen women and I arrived in Auckland in October of 1998. New Zealand was magical. The fresh air was crisp and clean. Everywhere we looked from the bus windows were beautiful green hills, magnificent mountains, thousand-year-old kauri tree forests, and fields of purple flowers. The Maori people of those beautiful islands captured our imagination, and we wanted to learn more. I couldn't wait to talk to them about their way of healing.

The Maori are Polynesian settlers of New Zealand who migrated there from islands of the South Pacific around AD 800. I had learned about the Maoris from Rangimarie "Rose" Turuki Pere, a well-known Maori leader, on her visit to Boulder, where she had greeted me with *hongi*, the traditional greeting of pressing noses. Her presence and wisdom in the Maori culture inspired all.

We headed south through amazingly green and beautiful land. Looking at hundreds of sheep grazing the hillsides filled me with peace. Nestled alongside nature's breathtaking vistas was an unusual and unique *marae*, a sacred village where Maoris live. We were given special permission to visit.

Marae villages enable Maoris to continue with their own way of life: to pray to a higher power, to have their feasts and festivals, to weep for their dead, to have weddings, to dance and sing, to know their own inherited culture. Indigenous world cultures have always inspired me with their belief in the sacredness of the earth and all beings.

We climbed out of the bus feeling respect and gratitude for the opportunity to visit. Waiting outside the entrance, we heard the *karangu,* or welcome call. A middle-aged man dressed in blue jeans and a white, flowing shirt approached and said, "Welcome. We appreciate your visit."

Should we greet him with hongi, the pressing of noses? I wondered.

A large man named Kaiko explained that the marae was a highly balanced feminine and masculine village. "We work to achieve the inner and outer balance within ourselves, holding each aspect in equal esteem," he said.

Like many American women, I have recognized and experienced how out of balance our Western culture is with its emphasis on patriarchal control. We, as women, are still learning that we don't need to be like men to be powerful, courageous, or intelligent. In the Maori culture, the values of compassion, connectedness, and empathy—what Western culture sees as "female" characteristics— are seen as necessary components of balance.

As we followed Kaiko on a tour of the village, he told us that it was laid out architecturally to follow the form of a woman. At the head was the library; the breasts held the nursery for children; the stomach was the kitchen; etc. As we finished the tour, I asked him what medicines they used for healing and how they healed emotional trauma.

I was fascinated by his reply. "We use very little medicine for illness," he said. "For emotional issues, indeed, if a person is sick in any way, including stress-related disorders, we start by calling the entire community, children included, to come together in the main hall. The person who is ill is placed in the center, and the rest of the community gathers around them. The healer asks one question, 'What is it that you are not saying?'"

"That's it?" I asked incredulously. He smiled, seeming somewhat amused with my question.

"Yes, we all wait until the person says what he or she had not revealed to anyone. Sometimes we wait for days until the person reveals all of what he or she is keeping to herself of himself. We believe that when we keep disturbing thoughts or experiences secret, we get sick."

"What is your cure rate with this procedure?" I asked.

"Around 90 percent," he replied. "When we hold our authentic feelings and thoughts inside of us, it can make us sick. It is also the quality of our listening, not so much the wisdom of our words, that is able to effect the most profound change in the people around us."

"The last person that was sick with a lingering cough and bad sore throat told the circle after a day of sitting and not saying anything that he was terrified of the silence he had sat in for months. He was the person in charge of communicating with other marae villages. He was afraid of feeling deeply within himself the suffering experienced by many poor Maoris. As he allowed their suffering in, within a few days his illness disappeared."

The Maori were using their own innate wisdom and inner guidance, the power of full self-expression, and interconnectedness: the heart of both the feminine and masculine values. The heart of healing was to be still enough to hear (not to make themselves heard) and to give thanks to those who voice their deepest truths. How different our American culture is, in which we try to be so independent and private, surely hindering our healing process.

The effects of healing often happen at a level below what scientists can measure. We do not have laboratory equipment that directly measures qualities such as love or intention. Yet we know that love and intention to heal are crucial.

The day following the visit to the village, I was sitting in a restaurant having breakfast with two of my women travelers. We were discussing dreams we'd had recently, and I had just had a dream where I was not listening to my own intuition. We remembered that Kaiku said that children were taught from an early age to trust their intuition. "The universe steps in to help when we get good at it," he said.

Suddenly I felt that something was terribly wrong at home in Boulder. My stomach quivered, and I felt a little nauseated. My friends encouraged me to call home before we left for our next destination. The front desk people allowed me to make the international call.

"Is everything okay there?"

"No, Mom," Shannon said. "Dad just had a car accident, and he is on his way to the hospital. That's all I know."

I could feel the bile rising from my stomach into my throat. *Listen to your own intuition, Chris!*

Arrangements were made for me to fly on a small airplane to Auckland. Before leaving, the women put me in the center of a circle and gave me blessings for my journey home and for David's healing. One woman gave me a sacred object that she had carried with her for a long time.

Their prayers sustained me during the short flight up to the international airport in Auckland. *I have to take my chances in finding a flight home to Denver. I have to go. My beloved husband is hurting, and I do not know the extent of his injuries. And Shannon is only sixteen and alone.*

I found my way to the United Airlines ticket window. The line was long, and I was exhausted with worry and travel fatigue. I explained that my husband had had an accident, and I needed to go home. The ticket agent curtly told me that I would have to pay double the price for a new ticket and wait two days for a flight. I broke into tears and felt myself getting panicky.

Suddenly I felt someone's arms around me and heard her gently telling the ticket agent that she would take care of the matter for me. She gently helped me to a lounge chair. I noticed she worked for United Airlines.

"I overheard you talking to the ticket agent," she said. "Sit here and drink this water while I talk to my manager. Can I have your tickets please?" A half hour later, she returned and told me, "You do not have to pay additional money for your emergency trip home. You can take a flight out at midnight tonight." It was noon at that time. She had found me an entire row of empty seats on the plane so I could sleep the sixteen hours on the flight home.

Looking at her with great humility and appreciation, I said, "You are my angel. Please tell me your name."

And she replied, "My name is Angel."

I looked at her in disbelief. I felt a tingling on my scalp. I had experienced this tingling on other occasions at times of divine intervention.

She invited me to go home with her and rest and to have dinner with her family until the midnight flight. She would then drive me back to the airport. I gratefully accepted. In moments like that, I know I am being guided, so I chose to trust her. That afternoon I slept in her daughter's bed and felt welcomed by her husband, son, and daughter.

During the dinner conversation, I mentioned that my husband and I had just written a medical directive for how someone could make their wishes known when approaching death. Angel was immediately astonished, because her mother was in the process of dying, and she had no idea how to handle it. Apparently New Zealand hospitals did not have good information about death and dying. I said I would send a copy to her as soon as I arrived in the United States. Angel was very grateful for this desperately needed assistance and knowledge.

The synchronicity of life and being there for other people when we need it is so inspiring to me. I had tears in my eyes when she dropped me off to catch my flight at the airport. We wrote regularly to each other over the years.

When I arrived home, I discovered that David was going to be okay; he had some bruises and needed minor knee surgery. A teenage driver had turned into David's lane, hitting his car and running it off the road into a large metal pole. The car was totaled, but David would recover.

Life presents us with such incredible kindnesses along with challenges. Angel helped me to be present to what was happening and made it safe for me to reveal my pain. I am also thankful for learning the Maori way of healing; it enabled me to reveal my pain to a stranger.

New Zealand stands out among the multitude of places and events that have shaped my life in many deepening ways. The healing way of the Maoris became imprinted in my brain. I learned how important it is to listen to my intuition. I marvel at the kindness of strangers. In the most unexpected ways, these experiences expanded my personal growth and planted a firm foundation for emotional trauma work and international service I would be doing in the near future.

Chapter 5

The Aloha Spirit

Being touched by love in any form brings healing.

Shivers ran through my body as I waited my turn to jump into the clear, cool, turquoise-blue ocean from the snorkeling boat. Eight other women from our New Millennium Women's Gathering were already in the water, swimming toward a pod of spinner dolphin off the Big Island of Hawaii in December 1999.

I had been snorkeling and scuba diving several times, so I wasn't afraid to participate—until I jumped off the boat and caught my thumb in a small metal ring. The ring and the force of my jump ripped a huge gash in my thumb. In the stinging salt water, intense pain moved through my hand. Disoriented, I noticed my thumb was bleeding profusely.

I swam over to Pat and held up my thumb as it bled into the water. "Pat, please help. I hurt my thumb when I jumped off the boat."

"I'll help you back to the boat," she said with dismay and concern in her voice.

Just then, a large dolphin appeared right next to me, making high squeaking sounds. This startled me at first, but then I sensed this dolphin was trying to help me. I extended my bleeding thumb toward this beautiful creature. "I'm in a lot of pain," I said. To my astonishment, the dolphin touched my thumb with her nose several times, as if she was softly caressing it.

I tried to stay calm, gulping in air, but I was astonished. I reached out and touched the dolphin's head tenderly and continued to tread water with my one available arm. The dolphin calmed me, and the water seemed warmer.

As the bleeding continued, I headed back to the boat, with the dolphin close behind. Pat helped me up the ladder, and breathless, I fell into the boat. I watched the dolphin swim away as several women on board, attended to my injury with a bandage over quite a large gouge in my thumb. My heart was still beating wildly, but I was so grateful to my dolphin friend.

Once back at the Dragonfly Ranch, we took the bandages off. To our surprise, it looked a lot better than it had on the boat. Looking up at my friends, smiling and waving my thumb at them, I exclaimed, "My dolphin did a great job!" The terrible aching had stopped, but my friends still thought I should have stitches.

My friend Bobbi enthusiastically told us that research on dolphins had shown that injured people experience healing with dolphins because dolphins somehow trigger the release of many healing chemicals in the body (from endorphins that relieve pain to interferons that help prevent cancer), leading to physical healing.

This new aloha experience added to my ever-growing knowledge of life's miraculous healing ways. *Aloha* is the breath of the ancient Hawaiians, not only meaning "hello" or "goodbye," but also a state of mind filled with compassion and gratitude.

That evening, I went to see Aunty Eliana, a Hawaiian woman with long gray hair, whom I had been told was a shaman of an ancient method of healing. In her small, modest cottage, I told her about my dolphin experience. "I think," she said with a twinkle in her eye, "that dolphins probably know of our ancient way of healing, called *ho'oponopona*."

"Please tell me about this way of healing," I said, sitting in a comfortable old chair, drinking the tea she had given me.

"It's a process and attitude that if you want to heal anyone or yourself, you first take responsibility for your life, because everything you experience *is* your responsibility—that is, anything occurring in your life is what you have manifested." She took a sip of her tea. "There is no guilt involved."

"As a psychotherapist," I replied, "I believe that most of what we all experience are our own projections, and I understand that we are all one and that separation is an illusion, but—"

Smiling gleefully, Aunty Eliana said, "If people want to experience less suffering, they have to heal themselves. In other words, the problem is with you and not anyone else."

"Can you tell me how it is done?" I asked.

"Say to yourself, 'I am sorry, please forgive me, I love you, thank you,'" she said. "And we are speaking to Spirit," she replied.

Aunty Eliana went on to say that in saying this over and over again, we evoke the spirit of love to heal within ourselves whatever is creating the outer circumstance.

"That's it?" I asked incredulously.

"*Aloha kekahi i kekahi,*" she said softly as she got up and took my tea cup out of the room. I quietly said, "*Mahalo,* Aunty Eliana," and left her cottage.

I found out later that the phrase translates "Love one another as you would wish to be loved." A few years later, after reading some books on the ho'oponopona method, I got good results myself for alleviation of my own suffering.

It is said that the ancient Hawaiians felt blessed and healed by the animals of the sea. Healing comes from love and compassion, from nature, from humans, from God, from your heart being touched by love. I learned this deeply from my retreat in Hawaii. A renewed part of myself was brought forward in the soft trade winds there. I felt a new sense not only of connection in relationship to everything but also of responsibility for this world and for myself without guilt or blame.

Chapter 6

Healing the Wounds of War

*Compassion for our own pain and the suffering
of humanity keep our hearts open.*

Peering through the windows of the airplane, I watched clouds begin to break. Below were the war-torn hills surrounding Skopje, the capital of Macedonia. It was the first week in September 1999, and we were flying toward Kosovo in the wake of another genocidal disaster. The Kosovar Multinational Peacekeeping Force (KFOR) of fifty thousand, led by an international NATO team, had just arrived in Kosovo. I arrived with a team of ten American psychotherapists supporting the international effort to work with refugees' emotional trauma and to teach alternative methods for healing their trauma.

While we waited for Albanian Kosovars to escort us to the border and help us cross on foot into Kosovo, my mind and heart wandered. I felt a tightening around my heart as I faced the unknown territory ahead, and all I could think was, *What am I doing here?*

One morning, several months earlier, I had watched a CNN report on the war in Kosovo. The president of Serbia wanted the rich land that the Kosovars were sitting on, and the Kosovars wanted independence from Serbia. Killing on both sides had occurred, as had the genocide of the Kosovar people. While watching the report, I got a phone call from Dr. Jim Gordon, an MD psychiatrist and the director and founder of the Mind-Body Medicine Clinic in Washington, DC. He asked if I wanted to be part of his international

Healing the Wounds of War project. Having told him earlier in the year that I was moved by his refugee work, I had answered yes without a moment's hesitation. I was answering a call deep within myself to help in some small way in this humanitarian effort, promoting a new way of healing by using alternative methods. As a psychotherapist and teacher in mind-body medicine for twenty years, I had to follow my inner instincts.

"Are you okay?" asked my colleague Carol, as I sat staring into space while waiting for our vans in Macedonia.

"Yes," I said. Then I confided, "I'm reviewing why I'm here so I can emotionally be of service the best way I can in this war-torn place."

"I totally understand," she said. "I'm doing the same to ground myself as well. It's imperative that we are able to be calm in the midst of intense suffering."

I could feel adrenaline flow through my body as fear welled up inside. *Will I be able to be calm enough over the course of the next three weeks? Will I be strong enough?*

We would be teaching Kosovar health care professionals to manage the stress and trauma of war in themselves and to teach these techniques to the people they would be serving in Kosovo. Jim's work was based on the idea that individuals and communities can best heal themselves after the trauma of war by learning and using the skills to do that. He had already worked in Bosnia and Macedonia with refugees.

In Prestinia, the capitol of Kosovo, the free training would be offered to 140 Albanian health care practitioners. We would use many alternative methods to work with emotional trauma, including biofeedback therapy, art therapy, meditation, autogenic training, visualization, movement therapy, and small group therapy. Our team would return every six months to work with the participants.

As streaks of pale pink light crossed the Macedonian sky, we finally set off in a couple of vans for the border, with the stark Sharr Mountains in the background. It was just weeks after Kosovar

Albanian refugees had returned by the thousands from Albania and Macedonia.

Stopping before the border crossing, we walked on foot into Kosovo. Dragging our one small piece of luggage over gravel and stones and wearing our backpacks, we saw soldiers with machine guns ahead. I looked around the bleak landscape, knowing that there were more land mines in Kosovo than anywhere else in the world. *Don't think of that right now. Keep going.*

After a two-hour drive, we entered Pristina and saw large military tanks, soldiers with machine guns, and mayhem on the hilly streets. It was apparent that KFOR had finally arrived in a delayed response to the genocide. *The help has come so late,* I thought. *Didn't they learn anything from the genocide five years ago in Bosnia?*

As we pulled up to the Grand Pristina Hotel, we could see that it was not so grand. It was, like the people, greatly in need of repair from the wounds of war. About a hundred feet to the right of the hotel, hundreds of Kosovars—young, old, and in-between—were marching up and down the main street with big smiles on their faces, many of them carrying the Kosovo flag, obviously celebrating their newfound freedom. I could feel in some way their relief over human rights being restored to them. It was truly an historic moment.

A small child was riding on his father's shoulders, grinning and waving red and yellow artificial flowers. Old women and young girls dressed in bright colors were part of the procession. The sun was shining, and the air felt electric with excitement as they crowded together, marching down several blocks of the street, turning around, and marching back again to our hotel. They continued this celebratory ritual for hours throughout the day.

Electricity at the hotel was sketchy at best. The Serbs had sabotaged two power plants in the province, and KFOR had managed to get one of them working only sporadically. The hotel was challenging, but we had a place to work and stay for the week.

The next day we met with our small groups in individual rooms after the morning lectures. I set up a circle of chairs around an altar, on which I placed flowers and beautiful stones. After people gathered and took their places, we opened with a blessing for all of us, inviting a collective intention to work together for healing. We remembered their lost loved ones, their eleven-year ordeal, and the loss of education for Albanian Kosovars.

After a moment of silence, one participant began his story. "My mother, father, and younger siblings finally left the refugee camp after several months and returned home," said Asad, a tall, middle-aged doctor. "They were surprised to find their home still standing, expecting it to have been burned to the ground like their neighbors' homes. In celebration, my mother and father made a simple meal to be eaten at their dining room table." He stopped and tried to stop the tears that were forming.

"What happened next, Asad?" I asked gently.

Sobbing, he continued, "I am embarrassed to break down like this, and I feel that my pain will never end if I let myself feel it."

"I understand," I replied softly. "However, when we struggle to contain our painful feelings, our hearts become heavy, and we tend to stop any new feelings that may arise. It is good to feel them all the way through and then release them so our hearts can open again."

"What my family did not know was that the Serbs had planted a bomb on the leg of my father's chair," Asad said through his tears. "After everyone sat down, he pulled out his chair, and the bomb went off, killing most of my family."

Tears fell silently in our tiny, dark room that day, as eleven Kosovars, my interpreter, and I felt Asad's pain and loss.

Every day for a week, we heard unspeakable, horrifying stories. The team taught methods of self-healing. And once individuals started to share, others felt safe to speak of their own pain and loss.

Hearing the participants describe gut-wrenching trauma, story after story, was anguishing. Yet the love and care given and received was palpable in the room. This was sacred listening, and sacred for everyone present. Somehow, even after horrific genocide, they were all tender with each other. Most participants carried intense anxiety that showed in their bodies: their hands and feet twitched and shook as their words tumbled out, and most were chain-smoking. This was the aftermath of extreme horror. The PTSD demonstrated there was beyond anything I had encountered before.

One evening, our group was invited to go through a Serbian neighborhood to have dinner with contacts that were helping our team to arrange travel to other cities in Kosovo. Our Albanian driver, Amir, and another guide, Zava, natives to Pristina, were in the front seats. My colleague Rob and I were sitting in the back. I felt a bit nervous, knowing we were driving through a dangerous area of the city. As the sun set, we saw burned-out apartment buildings, garbage piled up in the streets, and people furtively hurrying along.

"We have to stop for a roadblock," our driver whispered back at us, hissing urgently under his breath. "Remain silent; do not say a word." Men armed with machine guns surrounded the car and pointed their guns at all four car windows. The barrels of their guns seemed like evil eyes staring us down, only inches away from the windows. We were stunned silent, our eyes glued on the guns. Seconds passed. I took a breath and looked at Rob.

"Well, here we go, Chris," he whispered to me very softly, fear echoing in his words. I remember distinctly having a laser-like thought: *We may not make it through this.* My breath was fast and shallow.

Our driver, Amir, whispered again, "Do not say a word." Our guide, Zava, rolled down her window and began to speak Serbian. If she could convince them that we were Serbs visiting someone at the other end of the city, we might be okay to continue on. Apparently, she did convince them: they motioned us on. We exhaled and began to tremble as we realized the danger.

The team and I experienced powerful anger, grief, and sadness every day. We tried to stay present in the experience and release them with the help of our daily team debriefings. The violation of human rights was horrifying. Cultivating and maintaining compassion for the Serbs after hearing about the unspeakable violence Albanians had experienced at their hands was pushing me to the edge, even though I knew that, as with any war, brutality was perpetrated by both sides.

Part of our work was to travel around the province to help with children's war trauma. Driving in two Range Rovers through the Suharaka area, we looked out the windows for Serbian-laid land mines. The area had been hit very hard by bombings and fighting. Homes were bombed and left in ruins, with burned vegetable fields nearby.

Our team went into classrooms to work with the children, using mainly art therapy techniques to encourage them to express their feelings. The children shared desks and were crammed into small classrooms, and they did not have even paper or pencils. Seeing them smile with delight when we passed out paper and brightly colored crayons was gratifying.

"Is this a small animal in your picture that is being hurt?" I asked a timid six-year-old. "And is this you next to the animal, and is this someone who is shooting the animal?"

"Yes," he replied somberly.

His drawing was his way of telling the story of his father's death. The classroom teacher leaned over to me and whispered through an interpreter that many of the young children had witnessed the killing of their fathers. The fathers had been buried in the schoolyard without a proper Muslim burial.

Because of this information, our team moved the children into the schoolyard and performed a ritual next to the mass gravesite to ease their grief. Standing in a circle around the graves, we observed how the children kept their heads down, silent and still. The interpreter said some words of comfort in Albanian language.

At the end of that very long day, I found myself outside near the gravesite and next to the very old, rundown latrine shared by the entire school. I felt like I was in a wasteland bereft of any good. I collapsed in the dirt and leaned against the latrine. I sat there and sobbed with grief for our collective inhumanity and capacity for violence. I couldn't breath and was gasping for air through my sobs. Struggling to get through the pain, I could not manage to make any sense of the events I had been witnessing.

Then, in one sacred and holy moment, I received a healing, a presence of love that made me feel whole again. One of the little boys whose father had been buried in the schoolyard saw me crying and sat down quietly next to me. My eyes were still closed, so I did not know of his presence. I felt the soft touch of his finger on my cheek, wiping away my tears, and I opened my eyes. A trembling wave of release moved through me. His deep-brown eyes looking compassionately into mine became my eyes. We were one with each other.

That small gesture from the precious little boy made me feel safe, embraced with penetrating love, and held in the joy of God's presence. I was filled with an awareness of profoundly knowing that we all, every one of us, Serb and Albanian alike, are one. That moment of sacred sweetness, that generosity of spirit after all he had suffered, transformed me.

He sat with me in silence for a few minutes. I stood up, and he placed his little hand in mine as we walked toward the school. At the door to the school, he left me, not looking back. He had turned on the light in all the darkness I had felt. He had opened my heart wider so the pain could be held without me inwardly collapsing more. In the depth of pain, opening my heart even wider was absolutely necessary for healing.

To describe sacred moments like this is also to describe the shadow forces in life. That small boy wiping away my tears gave me strength and emotional stability right in the midst of terrible pain and grief. He was able to give a gesture like the Dalai Lama might give, like someone who had known pain and therefore knew compassion.

Most of us don't like to think about or even talk about the violence and the hatred in the world, for many reasons. One reason is that we understand how powerful and important it can be to focus on the positive and avoid the negative. I learned on a deep embodied level to stop pretending that life is supposed to be a certain way and to accept it on its own terms.

An Albanian man named Rahim stood out in our small-group sessions. He seemed to have come to a different place with himself and found some inner peace with the war. He was more tranquil than the others, and his energy provided focus and stability in the group. Rahim told his story readily, despite the strong grief that clearly still haunted him.

"I grew up in this city of Pristina, right next door to a Serbian family," he said. "And as two families, we had become best friends. The Serbian family had a boy the same age as me, and we grew up together—from the time we were small children until recently, when we were middle-aged men living side by side. Suddenly, in the spring of 1999, everything changed. These neighbors turned us in to the Serbian police. I was forced to watch as my mother was beaten and my father was brutally killed in my own home.

"I fled to the mountains on foot, where my wife, children, and I were hidden in the forest for four months before we returned to Pristina. While in hiding, I had some time to think about what had happened. I came to the conclusion that the betrayal of my family was part of the human condition."

Understanding his personal part in the human condition gave him enough perspective to find a broad kind of acceptance. The depth of that acceptance—not just saying it intellectually, but also actually experiencing it—allowed him to move to a place of strength that none of the others had been able to achieve. Many other people in the group could see this as well, and they commented about how starkly it contrasted with the emotional devastation they were still experiencing.

"How did you arrive at such an emotionally healthy place in the midst all the horrible tragedy around you?" I asked.

Rahim replied, eyes cast downward, in a quiet voice, "I asked myself one question over and over again, and one question only: How can I prevent this from happening to my own children?"

He realized that if he held onto the anger and bitterness and hate, it would only help to repeat the trauma he had experienced. He knew he had to let that go and start a new path.

By asking that question, Rahim was laying a foundation to build bridges between two ethnic cultures. This task of seeing our enemies, our own neighbors, as they are in the moment and not as we would like them to be, isn't easy. Can we learn to accept them anyway? I'll always remember this story and Rahim's single question: "How can I prevent this from happening to my own children?" This question has guided me, my family, and the many people I've continued to work with in countries around the world.

I was horrified, stunned, and shocked by these stories. Much of my experience came into perspective for me on the last day of our work when a middle-aged participant said, "This work you all did with us has made our suffering soften. You gave us hope and love for life and immortality, and all your teaching we will keep in our hearts and try to spread to others, in order to heal the wounds of our souls."

The stories we heard from Albanian doctors, nurses, and teachers allowed us to see that true healing comes from within. Our team realized that we could assist in the natural process of healing using deep listening and holy compassion. The adults and children that we worked with were facing their pain. They expressed it as authentically as they could. Perhaps we were in some small way helping to create a space in which the conditions that caused the violent abuse could start to unravel.

As we were leaving Macedonia on our way to Zurich, Switzerland, to debrief emotionally and physically for a couple of days, a flight attendant approached me and said in a huffy way, "You need to get up and move two rows back."

I replied, "This is my seat assignment."

"Well, you have to move," she insisted as she walked down the aisle.

I got up and moved, yet inside I was fuming, consumed with anger. I knew it had nothing to do with the flight attendant or the inconvenience of having to change seats. I was angry with the Serbs and the violence in the world. As soon as the "Fasten Seat Belt" sign went off, I walked down the aisle to find Jim and asked if we could talk. I told him about this incident and how disturbing it was to me that I was not feeling the neutrality that I wanted to feel.

"Chris," he said, "it is just human nature for you to be feeling angry after the horror of what we just experienced." This helped a great deal to contain my anger at human insanity.

When we look at the world today, we see a huge amount of hate expressed; yet at the same time, I believe there is more love than ever before. The refugees in Kosovo taught me that there was more hope, understanding, and desire for peace than ever. These two opposites—my simultaneous experiences of horror and hate as well as love and compassion—help me believe that humanity is growing closer to a world of cooperation.

Sometimes when we seem farthest away from peace, it is indeed the closest, like night being the darkest just before dawn. I learned that the real potential of suffering is for the victims to find compassion for and give support to one another. The situation in Kosovo was about the human condition—how we abuse each other and how we care for each another.

Encountering the evil that was perpetrated has been one of my greatest learning experiences. Truly, one task for healing in this new millennium is sharing our resources and enhancing aspects of one another's lives locally, nationally, and globally. This work opened my heart to a more expansive, inclusive, and compassionate embrace of the world.

Feeling deeply humbled by my experience, I found it easier to drop my prejudices and projections and to meet others' needs. The sensitivity that was needed for the horror that the refugees experienced opened me for more international work to come.

Since that time, the practitioners and recipients of the training have been using a variety of self-regulation and self-healing techniques and teaching them to their colleagues. Those colleagues are in turn using them in schools, hospitals, and clinics all over the province. Our data from the Healing the Wounds of War project shows that this multiplier approach works to heal emotional trauma and PTSD.

The colleagues that we worked with are now largely free from the intense emotional trauma and PTSD that they suffered from, and they now have happier lives. For me, it doesn't get any more rewarding than that.

Chapter 7

The Hero's Journey

Healing is about allowing your own vulnerability to be your strength.

The two-gallon pot of mashed potatoes that I had peeled, cooked, and mashed the night before felt very heavy as I lifted it out of the garage refrigerator., I thought, *I only have to carry it about eight feet to the kitchen door.* Suddenly, feeling dizzy, I lost my balance, and the potato pot crashed to the cold cement floor, scattering huge clumps on my feet. "Oh no!" I wailed, and I started to cry.

My youngest daughter, Shannon, came running and grabbed my arm to steady me. "Shan, what will we do now for the potatoes?" I whimpered. "We have sixteen people coming for Thanksgiving dinner today, and they expect mashed potatoes!"

"It's okay, Mom" she said. "I'll make new ones." I felt so relieved and thankful for her offer to help. (Actually, later that night after dinner, I realized that she had made mashed potatoes from a box!)

What is happening to me? I thought as Shannon helped me onto the living-room couch to rest. *My brain is not working correctly.*

As I rested on the couch, thoughts of the entire past year came crashing down on me just like the mashed potatoes. The severe and sudden reaction to the potatoes made me realize that the whole year had been full of traumatic incidents for me, and the potatoes were just a trigger. I had worked with refugees twice in Kosovo as well as in Israel. I was president of an international energy medicine society, and I had started a new position as a core professor at Naropa

University, all in addition to my psychotherapy practice. The tragedy of September 11 had happened just two months previously.

I was stopped cold and stunned that Thanksgiving Day, and tears rolled down my cheeks. The memory of all I had experienced overwhelmed me. I had continued to press ahead, not allowing myself the time to heal. As a therapist, I was well aware that PTSD often requires layers of healing, and my work was not finished.

The week before, I had chosen a simple LASIK operation on only one eye to help me with all the academic reading I had to do. My optometrist (who was not an MD) had told me that the surgery would help with my eyestrain problems. An eye surgeon from Kansas City would fly in to his Denver office and perform the simple outpatient surgery.

It sure didn't feel simple anymore, and I was feeling deeply confused and scared. After the surgery, I had made it through the end of the semester with dizziness and fatigue. I told the optometrist that I also had intense pain running from my right eye down to my shoulder and that both eyes hurt when I tried to read. Because my eyes hurt constantly, I had to become more creative with teaching, adding a lot of experiential learning to my classes. Fortunately, the new teaching method was very effective.

Each month the optometrist would say, "It will take a while for your eyes to adjust, and the complications will go away eventually." But the symptoms worsened. Through the spring semester, consulting doctors told me I must take a complete medical leave so my eyes could heal. I was devastated. My career and finances would be in jeopardy, but there was no other option. I also loved my students and the three classes I was teaching.

I discovered that the optometrist had been putting insufficient silicon into both corners of my eyes for the severe dry eye that usually results from LASIK surgery. Although it felt that my world was falling apart, I finally realized that I must take a medical leave from work and focus on healing.

It was a cold wintery day eight months later as I sat in my therapist's office. She asked how I was doing.

"Well, my energy reserves have been limited for a long time; it is still hard for me to read; I have severe pain in my right side of my neck; and I decline all social engagements," I replied. "I feel like I am adrift in the middle of a turbulent ocean."

"Chris, you have suffered physically, mentally, emotionally, and spiritually," she said quietly.

"Some days I feel so useless and helpless," I said. "And I've never felt such despair. I can't believe that I was minimizing the pain and denying my condition for all those months after surgery. I tried to appear normal, hoping that my eyes would get better, but in fact I was terrified and in big-time denial."

"Yes, but you took a powerful step for your own self-care and healing when you asked for the medical leave from everything— teaching, your clinical practice, and your volunteer work," Ann replied.

"It took me so long to realize what I refused to see—it made me feel so vulnerable and weak."

"You have spent most of your life taking care of others," said Ann. "It's time for you to let others take care of you. You have a history of several acute illnesses, like nephritis and hepatitis in your twenties and thirties. You healed very quickly then. This time it is taking much longer."

"I know this can be an opportunity for growth, but I'm devastated from feeling so disconnected from the goals and dreams I had. I feel guilty for choosing the surgery and for not realizing how I'd been hurt."

I was trying to allow myself to feel everything. I knew that being seen and accepted as vulnerable was a powerful lesson for me. The emptiness that I felt began to open up to a spacious darkness. *Could there really be light at the end of the tunnel?* I wondered. *How will I continue to live my life?*

Foolishly, we humans try to be in control of our internal and external worlds, and we crash when we see that we aren't in control at all. It is the illusion of the personality/ego identity, which provides a false sense of safety. And it certainly did not protect me from illness. How sick do we have to become to understand fully that our egos cannot order our worlds?

I was immediately afraid of becoming a burden to David. We had an empty nest, and he was going through his own process of figuring out what he wanted to do next. Work overseas? Retire from our medical center? Get board certified in hospice and palliative care?

During this period, the kids would call home from college and ask how I was doing. I told them I was seeing health care professionals—and not much else. I felt scared and incompetent and confused about who I was. I reached out to many of my friends and colleagues for help in recovering and was overwhelmed with their kindness and love for me. My women friends were total angels, and they provided a healing space for me to reveal my feelings. I was leaning gently into my pain, and I really felt how much I needed love and support.

With time, my embarrassment with being so vulnerable lessened, and I was learning to accept my weaknesses and be myself. Some of my old patterns were dying, making room for something new to be created. Part of me wanted to stay with this spiritual dark night of the soul rather than try to get rid of it.

I felt so much fear while in this dark place. I was seeking a deep and personal relationship with the Divine, with the Christ light. It was a test of my faith and trust. *How do I continue to find meaning and acceptance in my suffering?* was my daily question. I had never felt sick for that long. The depression I felt was overwhelming.

During that time, it felt good to come to terms with the truth of my condition and to tell others. In telling the truth, I felt more authentic and more intimate with others than ever before. It was important for me to make my needs known and to listen as others responded.

I started to surrender to exactly what was happening, to whatever God/Universal Intelligence wanted. At night, I sought alone time in our outdoor hot tub and prayed for guidance. The warmth of the water and the vastness of the sky above were soothing and transformative. I would pray aloud what I was grateful for, and I continued this ritual nearly every night.

In stories of the hero's journey in literature, the old identity gets stripped away in order for something new to arise. I gradually healed with the support of my friends and colleagues, and through alternative methods. I felt I was becoming more fully human through my time spent alone and facing darkness. I wanted to return once again to my life with compassion and wisdom.

One of my dear friends, Gladys McGarey, MD, who cofounded the American Holistic Medical Society, helped me with my impatience over the length of the healing process. I had met her twenty-five years ago at our annual Council Grove meetings on consciousness and healing, and I love and respect her deeply. During a telephone conversation, after listening to me complain, she told me a story:

> There was a man who was watching a cocoon, and he saw that the butterfly was just about to emerge. With great concentration and concern, he watched this cocoon. A little crack appeared in the cocoon, and a little bit of wing came out, but that was all.
>
> He thought, *There must be some way that I can help.* So with a great deal of compassion, he took a pair of tiny scissors and cut the cocoon just a little bit. The butterfly got a little bit more of itself out. He cut it more, and finally the butterfly emerged.
>
> When it emerged, its belly was swollen and its wings were shriveled. The butterfly was never normal, because it did not go through the struggle

of working to emerge from the cocoon, which would force that food from its belly into its wings as it emerged. The man's great concern and compassion had interfered with the natural process of unfolding.

"So, Chris," Gladys said, "be in acceptance of the struggle and pain that accompany what shows up in your life. With time and patience, this natural process will turn you into a beautiful butterfly."

In the hero journey, we come back into the world healed and ready to share our gifts and lessons. Coming back into the world after a year's medical leave from three positions, I started back with part-time work. I enrolled in One Spirit Interfaith Seminary (OSIS), which I could do at home online, listening to webinars, and traveling to New York City a few times a year for retreats and residential classes. I wanted to go deeper—deeper with God, deeper with noticing my own ego responses to life's process and choosing more often to respond from my higher self.

I felt different, and "new" in so many ways, with a relaxation and appreciation of life that I had not experienced before. My body was a lot happier.

The OSIS faculty taught the deep truths found at the heart of the many different spiritual traditions: compassion, wisdom, love, peace, and service. My own faith deepened profoundly. We were taught to explore our inner life in order to go out into the world to serve as ministers in some way.

After two intense years of study, during which I continued to teach and see patients at our family medical center, I was ordained as an interfaith minister in the magnificent and sacred Riverside Church in New York City. I could feel the presence of grace and love that embraced all of us in the graduating class. The beauty, the holiness, and the vows we took stayed with me as my ministerial work took me into hospital chaplaincy, spiritual direction, officiating at weddings and memorial services, and inspirational interfaith talks and dialogues.

What I took away from this journey from darkness into healing was the deep sense that healing is possible when we allow our vulnerability in. What really changes us in our day-to-day experience is the power of our thoughts and the honest way we face our struggles.

The Christian mystic St. John of the Cross said, "Our dark nights are times of sheer grace." Healing our inner judgments and negativity makes authentic and long-lasting change possible. To truly be of service in this world today, I want to serve and also take care of myself at the deepest level. Vulnerability is not a weakness. It is a foundational strength. I felt I was ready to go back into the world.

Chapter 8

Trauma in the Middle East: Women Reaching Out for Harmony and Understanding

*Releasing trauma that blocks connection
to ourselves and others is vital.*

Habiba, an Israeli Jew, head covered in a blue scarf, eyes cast down, walked haltingly into the room where I was working. She was one of a group of women who had been working for peace between Israelis and Palestinians. It was made up of Israeli and Palestinian women of Muslim, Jewish, and Christian faiths. I had given a talk to this group earlier in the day on PTSD (post traumatic stress syndrome) and a new approach to help resolve it, called EMDR (eye movement desensitization and reprocessing).

With EMDR, when a person recalls a painful incident, bilateral stimulation is applied with an instrument that moves his or her eyes from one side to the other. When the person focuses on the disturbing memory, emotions are desensitized, and he or she is left with the memory but not the traumatic energy around it.

Not surprisingly, whenever there is war, unresolved trauma is held in the human body. This trauma is stuck energy that has not been discharged. When new fearful events happen, they rekindle previously unresolved emotional trauma, reopening memories of past loss, hurt, and fear. A real or perceived threat triggers a whole-body sense of ongoing danger. This is not only a painful recurrence of trauma, but also fertile ground for intolerance for the other as well as a desire to strike out.

This group of women had been working in some way to encourage Israeli and Palestinian people to work together for mutual understanding and peace. It was not an easy task: each often looked at the other with suspicion. They had come together to bridge the differences in their cultures at a time when feminine empowerment was awakening on the planet. Habiba worked with Israeli Jews to bring families together.

I asked Habiba to sit in a comfortable chair and to try to relax her body. Facing each other, we began to breathe slowly and evenly together.

"Would you like to work on a specific incident today?" I asked.

"Yes," she said, with tears welling up in her eyes. "I woke one morning to the sound of bombing very close by. Terrified, I ran outside to see if I should move my little brother and grandmother to safety. I started to run to the Israeli headquarters a block away to determine what to do." Suddenly I was stopped by several Muslim teenage boys who surrounded me." She could hardly speak through her tears.

"Where do you think you are going?" they asked threateningly.

"I am going to Israeli headquarters down the street," I replied.

"So you think," one replied, dragging her behind a building. "It is because of you that Lebanon is bombing here!" he shouted.

"Then they yelled at me and pushed me to the ground," she tearfully replied. "I can't sleep because I have nightmares about that." Then she cried, "Why did they blame this on me?"

"War makes people crazy," I whispered sadly. "And war seeks to release tensions of fear through horrible violence. I am so sorry this happened to you. Let's do some work to help you desensitize this awful memory."

That day I worked with story after story of trauma incidents from both Israeli and Palestinian women. They had endured violence and many traumas along the way, but they continue to have a vision for all people to be treated equally.

Rachael's story was horrifying. Her parents were practicing Jews, but she did not practice Judaism in a religious sense. She entered the room confidently, ready to do some work. "I want to talk about a Palestinian suicide bombing that took place across the street from me," she said. "I was sitting outside at a coffee house, one warm, sunny day, talking to a friend, when a young Palestinian boy approached the outdoor vegetable market across the street. Many people were shopping there."

Rachael started to cry and was silent for a minute, trying to regain her voice. "Suddenly we heard a loud explosion and felt pieces of wood, vegetables, and body parts hit us. My friend and I threw ourselves onto the floor and stayed there until someone asked if we were okay. I stood up and looked across the street. Dead bodies were everywhere, and many people were missing hands and legs and were screaming. I froze and could not move for some time. Can you help me, because I still have nightmares about this incident?"

Rafit, another women from the group, also asked for help, saying, "The fear I carry is from an incident that happened not to me, but to my younger cousin. I am still having nightmares from this, and I am fearful to walk anywhere in the West Bank.

"My cousin had been admiring my work for peace and decided to stand up for herself and make some changes. But she comes from a very conservative Muslim neighborhood. One day she was walking in her West Bank neighborhood to get some groceries and did not have her headscarf on." Rafit started sobbing.

When she was able to continue, she said, "My cousin put on her headscarf, went through an Israeli checkpoint, and then removed the scarf, stuffing it into her pocket. She hated wearing it, as she felt inferior to other women who were not forced to wear one. She was almost to the grocery store, but before she put on her scarf again, several Arab men stopped her."

"Who do you think you are, walking around without your veil

on?" they shouted. "Girls like you need to be punished!" She felt the hot, painful burn of battery acid hit her face. She screamed, and people from the store ran out to help her as the angry men ran off. I was called and took my cousin to the hospital and stayed with her during treatment."

Rafit was carrying her cousin's horrifying trauma in her own body, what we call secondary trauma. You do not have to be in the traumatic scene at the time; you can carry the trauma from just hearing the stories.

My heart ached for Rafit, and I so admired her courage along with the courage the other women possessed. All of them held trauma that went back for centuries. Some were deeply religious Muslims, and some were Bedouins carrying the habits of their tribes. Some had political viewpoints that carried strong emotions.

Some were Christian Arabs with children and careers. Others were evicted from their homes by occupying forces. Some Jewish women were raised in prejudiced families and were not getting their families' support for their peace work. Many of their families found it difficult to accept their daughters' association with the "other."

Stories were told of village elders who felt threatened by the women's activities on behalf of other women. Even though Arabs and Israelis live close to one another, most groups seem to have no social connection. Many Arabs feel that they are feared as potential suicide bombers. Both groups come from very different cultures, even though they reside in the same area of land.

The women in our group had two different languages, but enough women understood enough Hebrew, Arabic, and English to understand each other's emotions and beliefs. When asked what tied them together, these women often answered, "Death."

Working with Israeli-Palestinian conflict in particular requires many creative therapeutic tools. These women experienced the use of dance, music, and art, and the principles for understanding ongoing trauma. I have witnessed the conscious and unconscious impact of collective trauma on groups and some of the social, political, and cultural aspects that go along with it. One of the most useful approaches to begin with is the telling of one's story, of the darkness and of the hope. Violence, terror, occupation of land, and a range of emotions was revealed, including hate, vengeance, anxiety, guilt, empathy, compassion, and love.

In one group discussion, it became clear to me that the Christian Palestinians were being guided by what the Holy Bible tells us: "Blessed are the peacemakers for they shall be called sons of God" (Matthew 5:9). The Israeli Jews were demonstrating what the Talmud tells us: "What is hurtful to yourself do not do to your fellow man" (Talmud, Shabbat 31a). And the Muslim women were practicing what their Holy Quran says: "Not one of you is a believer unless he desires for his brother that which he desires for himself" (Forty Hadith of an-Nawawi 13).

These remarkable Middle Eastern women were victims of unresolved trauma from the horrific effects of war and conflict. They had struggled to bring peace to a land in turmoil and were building bridges between those grieved by the loss of loved ones in a centuries-long battle. They did not want revenge. They wanted to transform themselves and understand each other.

All the women had been working tirelessly in different ways to encourage women to be strong. One had started the first-ever women's party in an Arab town, putting up a roster of women candidates for public office. Another had started sex education for Muslim girls in school. An Israeli Jew had set up interfaith theater for women. They all seemed to have been strengthened in many ways by hardship, and great courage shone through. Through it all, these peace activists kept working to ease the conflict between the Palestinian and Israeli people on a daily basis.

After many days together, we all sat in a circle. Tears fell as I looked around and saw love for one another streaming from their eyes. Each one had shared her family stories, her pain, fear, and heartaches, and her desire to transcend the hatred so prevalent in their societies. When they heard the pain of the other and recognized the other as another human being, suffering just as they were and wanting to live in peace with their neighbors, deep healing could take place. Yet at times the women could be quite angry at each other, and we were not sure how things would end.

Out of that shared pain and healing arose determination to care for each other. Some of the women, mostly the Palestinians, were encountering non-Muslim, non-Christian spiritual practices for the first time. We hoped that the strong bonds being made would bring more people together in the Middle East. These women refused to accept violence and chose to take responsibility to be involved in action toward peaceful change. By promoting respect and understanding, they have an opportunity for leadership toward community and service for the benefit of all people in the Middle East.

I felt privileged to be part of their visions for peace. I was doing my small part to help release and transform the traumas of living in a war-torn land. We all wish for mental and emotional stability, yet the continuing unresolved trauma in the Middle East is so troubling at this time. Palestinians feel they have been betrayed by their own leaders and see their children growing up oppressed and feeling like second-class citizens. Jews have felt oppressed for centuries and carry enduring memories of massive genocide. Both peoples are deeply traumatized.

The cycle of violence can be stopped by Israeli-Palestinian cooperative projects already in motion in schools and neighborhoods. Practitioners from emotional trauma, psychotherapy, mediation, social work, and education need to continue to come together to explore these avenues of healing.

Working with the Israeli and Palestinian women, I learned that being together and listening to one another can bring great understanding. Working with trauma that each culture has experienced as well as mediation in groups is essential. The complexities from such a long history between the two groups are great.

It was another clear lesson for me to understand that blaming the other never works. Being responsible and accountable for our own anger and actions as well as acting with compassion and empathy toward others are the only ways to reach out to others for harmony and peace.

Chapter 9

Pilgrims of Peace

*Service to each other unites and heals, removing
boundaries around our hearts.*

The pilot announced our descent into the city of Damascus. I gazed
out my window at the desert and hills surrounding the ancient land
of Syria. Full of hope and anticipation, I also felt apprehensive. Was
I really going to the land of biblical stories from my childhood?
Humans first walked in Syria ten thousand years before Christ. I was
awed by the prospect of visiting the oldest continuously inhabited
city in the world, yet I felt uneasy wondering how we would be
received. I decided to expect the unexpected.

In April 2005, international peace workers Elias Amidon and
Rabia Roberts invited David and me to travel with fifteen others
from different countries on an interfaith pilgrimage of peace. We
would start in Damascus and then go north to the ancient monastery
of St. Moses the Abyssinian.

"Why are you going to Syria?" asked the heavily bearded man
across the aisle from me in a rough voice. I wondered, *Is he angry, or
does he just have a raspy voice?*

"The purpose," I replied, "is a pilgrimage of peace, an opportunity
for our group of Western religious and community leaders to meet
with Syrian religious and government leaders, university professors,
and citizens in a cross-cultural exchange. We want to build bridges
of understanding between diverse faiths of East and West. People

of Western countries, particularly the United States in recent years, have had little contact with or understanding of Syria and the Syrian people."

The man looked away and said nothing. I felt a bit uneasy with this interchange. This type of lack of contact was contributing to the growing political unease and suspicion between Syria and Western nations and was occurring at a time of increased tensions between the Muslim world and the largely Christian West: between religious worldviews as well as between national identities and policies.

As I write now about my experiences while in Syria in 2005, much has changed. It was a peaceful country I experienced then. Now there is violent unrest with grassroots protest against the repressive government and the violence of ISIS. The civil war that started in 2011 has lasted over five years.

At the beginning of the twenty-first century, an evolutionary change in religious and spiritual values was moving toward a more global dimension of ethical, religious, and spiritual awareness. Many of us hoped that we could embrace peace and stewardship, demonstrating compassionate service in the face of human need.

As our plane landed, I wondered how Syrian citizens would describe their views of East-West conflicts and their visions of how real peace and mutual respect might be established. I was eager to deeply *listen* to both Muslims and Christians in their homes, mosques, and monasteries.

Bayon, our friendly young Syrian guide dressed in blue jeans and a cowboy shirt, met us at the airport and drove us to the small Majid Hotel, a block from the old city. I smelled the fragrant purple flowers growing up the hotel walls in the courtyard; turquoise and white tiles adorned those walls. After getting settled in our modest rooms, we ate the first of many delicious Middle Eastern meals at the hotel café.

We discussed our pilgrimage goals over spicy hummus, goat cheese, and aromatic tea. Our group goal was to acknowledge the cultural differences and misunderstandings between the Middle

East and the West. We would spend time at Muslim and Christian holy sites within Damascus and meet with Syrians to learn about their culture. To complete our three-week stay, we would stay at a monastery built in the eleventh century.

The muezzin's call to prayer came over crackling loudspeakers, as it did five times a day. That first night, I woke up at three in the morning to a hauntingly beautiful voice streaming prayers through the open window. My soul awakened that night, and five times each day thereafter, praying with my own prayers for healing and peace for all people.

The next day, Elias led us on a tour of the Old City, where we walked through narrow streets of ancient stone and wood houses with very small doors, on our way to the Umayyad Mosque. We stopped at the Hamidiyeh Souk, a huge, crowded, ancient bazaar that sold clothing, food, spices, and household furnishings.

The Umayyad Mosque was one of the most sacred and magnificent buildings of Islam. Sadly, it was largely destroyed during heavy fighting in 2013.

As we entered a huge rectangular courtyard with blue and white tiles, men were washing their feet at a special fountain in preparation for worship. Women were required to put on a long, dusty-green cloak with a head veil. The cloak and veil were hot and cumbersome. We walked around and found a place on the green, carpeted floor to do our own prayer work. All sacred places are holy to me, no matter the religion.

The mosque had been a temple to Jupiter and then a basilica dedicated to John the Baptist, whose head is said to be contained in a casket near the center of the mosque. I went over to peer into the casket, expecting to be frightened by a two-thousand-year-old skull, and much to my relief, the casket was closed.

The next day, we wandered around on our own in Damascus, with the purpose of initiating conversations where we could ask questions about Syrian's feelings and beliefs. David and I approached two middle-aged men dressed in dark suits, standing on a corner, talking. We approached them smiling and said hello, *marhaba*, in our minimal Arabic.

"Welcome to Syria!" they both said in perfect English, as they could tell we were Americans.

"Do you know where we can get some tea?" we asked. "We are visiting from America." They invited us to join them down the street at their favorite teahouse and introduced themselves as Nicola, a Christian, and Yaman, a Muslim. They were both professors at the University of Damascus.

Once we had settled into a corner table in the cozy little café and told them about the purpose of our pilgrimage, I asked them, "Did you ever have a dream as a child, and did that dream come true for you?"

"Yes!" said Nicola enthusiastically. "I always wanted to be a teacher, and I am now a professor at the university. What an interesting question to ask." Yaman said he had wanted to visit Europe and learn its history ever since he was a little boy. But he had never traveled out of Syria.

We talked for two hours, drinking tea and hearing about their dreams and desires for peace. We asked them what would they like the people of the West or the United States to know about Syria and the Syrian people. Yaman said, "We are dissatisfied with both the Syrian government and the American government. We would like to see the United States and all countries abide by the United Nations resolutions and withdraw from Occupied Territories." Yaman was very concerned that the United States would go to war with Syria because there were American troops already in Iraq.

"Syria is a house for visitors from everywhere," he continued. "We wish the government would do more to promote tourism."

"Come visit Syria, and see the oldest people in the world," said Nicola enthusiastically. "One big difference between the West and the East is in caring for the elderly. There are no nursing homes in Syria, because the families take care of their elders." He felt that

Western cultures had abandoned their elders, something unthinkable in Arab culture.

We thanked our hosts warmly for spending time with us and sharing tea. I believe they felt our friendship in return, because they asked to exchange contact information with us.

We visited churches, mosques, Sufi shrines, schools, homes, and Christian monasteries over the next three weeks. Our task was to listen and to try to understand, even though we did not necessarily agree with everything people said.

We met a grand *mufti*, one of Syria's most respected Shiite clerics. He met with us to discuss interfaith relations. Our organizers, Elias and Rabia, had met with this cleric on previous visits. The sheikh said he appreciated our Western view, which reflected our respect for their long and sophisticated culture, their commitment to family life, and their generous kindness.

"We all want to protect our children—in every culture. When we truly meet each other, we will have peace," he said.

We also heard from many Syrians about their anger at and suspicion of Americans. For thousands of years, empires have come to conquer their land and people. With the American occupation of Iraq on their eastern border and Israel's occupation of the West Bank and the Golan Heights—former Syrian territory—it was understandable that many Syrians might fear that American-Israeli interests have ideas about invading their land.

In a visit later in the week with another sheikh, who was the director of a large Muslim social service organization, we were told,

> There will not be peace in our world until there is peace among the religions. And there will not be peace among the religions until adherents come to understand one another. Muslims, Christian, and Jews all want peace and harmony. But we have been taught different things. It is important to listen to one another. There is a great future for this part

of the world if the religious traditions learn to cooperate to achieve these expressed goals.

Later that day, we were all escorted to a mosque to hear a sermon given by the sheikh. The women were instructed to sit in the balcony, and the men were escorted to the main hall. Listening to the sheik speak in Arabic to his people—about five thousand present—I was disturbed by the gruff, shouting tone of his speaking voice. (Through our headsets, we heard the English translation of his speech.)

Afterward, we were invited to his family villa, forty-five minutes outside of Damascus near the mountains. He and his wife were very gracious hosts, and I felt I might be able to approach him with my question. I asked a bit nervously, "I was surprised at your loud, gruff speaking voice in the sermon. Is this the way you always talk to your people?"

He looked at me searchingly while I squirmed, and then he said, "That is a good question. I do not like shouting, but it is the way of our religion. If I did not speak in a gruff voice, my people would think I was weak and ask for another person to be head of the mosque."

I nodded as if I understood but was confused. *Why do they intimidate their listeners?*

The next morning, we were on our way to the Golan Heights. It was a militarily sensitive zone occupied by the Israelis; UN forces occupied the border. Quneitra had once been a city of fifty thousand people and the administrative center of this area. By the time we arrived, most buildings had been flattened, either razed or bulldozed by the Israelis upon withdrawal in 1974 after occupation during the Yom Kippur War.

We stopped at the former Golan Hospital, now a shell piled high with rubble, pockmarked with bullet holes and rocket strikes. Our guide told us that Israelis destroyed the hospital after they evacuated the town. *Why don't they rebuild it?* I wondered.

From there we drove on to Beit Ajem with our Syrian guide to visit the founder of an Islamic nonviolence movement, one of the first Syrians to speak out. We were told that he was a philosopher and theorist educated in Syria and Egypt and that he represented the intellectual side of Islam.

His niece interpreted for him as he warmly invited us to sit down to have tea. He told us he was working not only on Islamic nonviolence, but also on environmental issues. He was obviously a visionary. At one time, he was jailed and considered dangerous for speaking out about nonviolence.

We asked him, "Do you think it is human nature to respond violently to violence?"

He emphatically replied, "Certainly not. Human nature does not respond to violence. You cannot coerce the human heart. Persuasion and compassion are what humans respond to. The universe is based on justice, and from those fruits you shall know it."

"What about the young people today and what are they being taught in Syria?" another member of our group asked.

"War is dead. Give this idea to the kids. Only the uneducated or the exploiters wage war. We all need to work against war. Humans will arrive at peace. You can change people's ideas with knowledge of history. The European Union is a new threshold in human history. The countries that warred forever are now coming together in a new evolutionary step."

We hoped that what he said was true and that we will all evolve to this. I wonder now if he could have envisioned at that time the terror and horror that was about to happen to his people.

Syrians, almost without exception, were universally friendly, generous, good-hearted, and genuinely interested and appreciative of our purpose. The pilgrimage allowed me to drop my own judgment and fear, to endeavor to truly meet the "other," and to realize that they are not "other" at all. Reaching across to others ultimately leads us to our own truth.

Chapter 10

Removing Walls Around Our Hearts
at the Deir Mar Musa Monastery

*The true nature of humanity is woven out of
the fabric of sacred love and goodness.*

We sat as equals in a circle on the worn, red carpet of the small ancient bBasilica at the Deir Mar Musa Monastery, built in the 16th sixteenth century, on the steep side of a mountain west of Damascus. Father Paolo sat with us on the purple cushions and asked our group of peace pilgrims if we had any questions. My question to him was, "What is the real power in the message of Jesus?"

He replied, "Jesus taught love and forgiveness of self and others. If we believe and practice this, we will know God."

Deeply struck by the power of this simple message, I was reminded again why millions of people worldwide have worshipped Jesus for over two thousand years. In this circle, I felt cradled in, wrapped in, and nurtured by God's presence. The breathtaking gold, red, and blue frescoes painted by monks a thousand years ago leaped out at me. The basilica held me in its heart, with its close vaulted ceilings and soaring archways between narrow rows of square stone columns. This sacred candlelit space held us and invited us into the presence of Christ's light.

Father Paulo, the director and senior priest, told us the original basilica was built in the eleventh century, was abandoned in the nineteenth century, and lay in ruin for 150 years until he arrived from Rome in 1982. Originally, this site overlooked a north-south route for travelers going to and from Turkey.

In the sixth century, the Ethiopian prince, Moses of Abyssinia, who gave up his claim to that throne, arrived and began a tradition of Christian hermits who lived in caves. These men prayed and wove blankets and mats of goat hair.

"During a ten-day retreat," Father Paulo said, "the Spirit moved me so deeply that I decided to rebuild the monastery." He continued to tell us that the basilica was built to face due east, so light from the rising sun would come through a special window at the time of the winter equinox. As we listened, sunlight streamed in, illuminating the cross opposite the equinox window. The restored frescoes showed the birth of Christ and His ascension to heaven.

The monastery consists of several structures built into the side of a mountain. It is situated in high-desert cliffs and accessible only on foot. Upon arrival, we ascended the long, steep path to the buildings, as our baggage was transported by an ancient trolley system. At each switchback, we had spectacular views across the vast plains eastward toward Iraq. *This is rough terrain,* I thought. *I hope I can keep up with the strenuous climbing that will need to be done over the next five* days.

Father Paolo was a handsome giant of a man who smiled often. He reached out to the local Muslim people in a deep and sincere way. He attended Muslim ceremonies in town below the monastery and invited them to come to the monastery to build religious understanding, acceptance, and celebration of each other's faith. He was well known throughout Syria for his successful interfaith efforts.

According to Father Paolo, desert monks studied how thoughts can interrupt a prayer field, inhibiting the real work of the heart. It sounded to me as though they were creating new neural pathways with prayers so they could live more fully from the heart, something we in the West are just beginning to discover.

Our days were filled with prayer and sewing together prayer flags that would be stretched across the gorge between the old and new parts of the monastery, which were linked by a crude, fifteen-foot suspension bridge. The monks engaged us in discussions of spiritual activism and service.

When I could slip away, I sought silent refuge in sacred caves among the rock walls. I loved praying alone in the caves and in the basilica, sometimes with Muslims who traveled up the mountain to join us.

One morning we overheard visiting Muslims discussing the mass Father Paolo had just celebrated.

"How do you feel about praying in this ancient Christian house of worship?" I asked them. I wondered how they would regard the Christian imagery on the murals. A tall, bearded man who looked to be in his late twenties spoke up in halting but understandable English, smiling from head to toe. "I get so inspired by the devotion of these monks, and I learn so much. I have been coming now for many months. I hear God's guidance here every time I come. Father Paolo's plan is to have us all live here in the harmony of God's love." The rest of the group nodded.

"Father Paolo is so open and balanced, especially for a Catholic priest from Rome. He is clearly aware of the fragility of the peacemaking process within the three Abrahamic religions in the Middle East." An older man named Hamid said, "We are concerned for his safety sometimes, when Muslims from Damascus come through this part of the country. Some of them have expressed their disfavor with this monastery."

This turned out to be true. In February 2012, around thirty masked and armed men arrived at the monastery, entered the basilica, and forced the people into a corner. The armed men apparently destroyed all means of communication that they found and searched for weapons. (The monastery had no guns, as they are dedicated to nonviolence.)

Last year, due to the civil war, the Syrian government asked Father Paolo to leave. He wrote in a monastery newsletter, "The very fact that I was in favor of change, human rights and dignity: this is very provocative." When the antigovernment demonstration began in 2011 and the civil war started, Father Paolo supported the young Syrians who risked their lives to protest peacefully. He immediately was sent a one-way ticket out of the country. It is reported that he was killed before he left.

In 2005, we experienced tolerance and acceptance in Syria between Christians and Muslims, a mutual existence that had lasted for hundreds of years. There seemed to be a communal desire to reach out to the other. Because Syria was 15 percent Christian—and Damascus, with six million people, was almost 25 percent Christian—we found churches alongside mosques in many neighborhoods. It was a model of peaceful coexistence and mutual respect at that time.

On our way home, leaving customs at the Denver airport, we wearily came out of an elevator only to be stopped by a man dressed in a baseball cap and shorts. He said, "You have come a long way from Damascus."

I concluded that he must have been on our flight, but we had had a two-day stopover in Austria, so how would he know this? I replied, "Yes, we are very tired. How do you know that we were in Damascus?"

"I am paid to know these things," he said. "Why were you there?"

At this point, I started to get nervous, as I wondered if he was CIA. "We were there as part of a peace mission," I said politely. "But then, you would know that." We walked quietly away, stealing a glance back to see if he was following us, but he was gone. We knew tensions in Syria were high and leaning toward civil war.

I wondered as we wearily drove home, *Can people ever let go of the "I'm right, you're wrong" game and open to the possibility for peace? When will we as a global community learn to let go of violence and judgment enough to pray together for the benefit of all?*

My heart cries out for all Syrians that have been jailed, tortured, and killed, especially the women and children. Now, at the beginning of 2016, the Syrian war has dragged on for over five years. Almost 250,000 lives have been lost, and 11 million people have been uprooted from their homes. Millions of refugees have made long, arduous trips to surrounding countries, leaving Europe overwhelmed. The war has led to the rise of the Islamic State, and Syrian President Assad still will not step down to end the civil war.

Humanity's mission, just like the mission of Dar Mar Musa, is to love and to meet the other. Jesus was constantly with people who were "the other": tax collectors, people of different beliefs, prostitutes, etc. We are all united in reaching for God, whether we are Christians, Muslims, Jews, or of other beliefs. We can seek to be kind and respectful. Surely this is what God wants—for us to love one another.

The pilgrimage allowed me to drop my judgments and fear, to endeavor to truly meet "the other," and to see that they are not "other" at all. We return to the common business of caring for each other. Being of service to each other unites us, removes walls around our hearts, and heals whatever divides us. As Gandhi said, "I'm not doing this for others; I'm doing this for myself."

Chapter 11

African Compassion and Forgiveness

Healing through forgiveness is one of the greatest gifts we give.

As we circled over the teal-blue waters of Lake Victoria, the butterflies in my stomach anticipated our landing. I had been to Israel and Syria and had learned so much about human struggle. There I was, in my beloved Africa once again, only this time in Uganda, a country I had never visited.

As we walked into the Entebbe airport, I felt great relief that machine guns weren't pointing at me as they had been thirty years before during a layover on my way to Kenya. President Idi Amin had been on the warpath at that time and was later found guilty of many crimes against humanity.

I got a sense of the location of this country, seeing it in my mind's eye on the global map, with Sudan to the north, Kenya and Tanzania to the east, Rwanda to the south, and the Congo, with its majestic Ruwenzori mountains, to the west. I looked around at the flame-colored tulip trees, the mangoes, and the colorful turacos flying from tree to tree. I felt gleeful and could not stop grinning.

"Ki kati! [Hello!]," exclaimed an airport guide in the Luganda language, although the official language of Uganda is English.

I responded with one of the phrases I knew, *"Oli otya?* [How are you?]"

"You are most welcome here!" he replied. It turned out that our main piece of luggage had not arrived, and it never did. But this was Africa.

David and I were there to visit our oldest daughter, Devin, and her husband, Mark, during the year they were living in Kampala. Devin had cofounded a nonprofit that benefited extremely poor women, most of whom were HIV-positive and widowed. The women made jewelry out of recycled paper that was sold in the United States. By selling us their beaded jewelry, they earned capital, which helps them start their own small business. Mark was finishing his master's thesis in conservation education and had scheduled a safari for us to Murchison Falls National Park.

The streets of Kampala, littered with garbage and potholes, were difficult to maneuver, but Devin drove through the city deftly. Early one morning, we visited a slum of Kampala. We walked along narrow alleys between mud-brick homes and were greeted by the shouts of young children playing in the dark-brown dirt. Some of them wore rags, and others wore nothing.

Emaciated stray dogs and garbage were everywhere, as were streams of dirty water from outdoor spigots; there was no indoor plumbing. The tiny houses were packed together, each with only one or two rooms. Corrugated metal roofs absorbed and radiated the merciless heat of the equatorial sun. We sweated profusely in the oppressive heat.

We arrived at the home of a newly enrolled beadmaker. Julie and her six children lived in one room, and mattresses covered most of the mud floor. Her worldly possessions—a few pots and pans, and a worn leather suitcase with some clothes tumbling out—were piled on a mattress. Two wooden chairs stood by a small window, which emitted very little light; the entire room was gloomy and dark.

Eliana, a widow in her forties, had a hacking cough. David thought she might have multidrug-resistant tuberculosis. "What do you enjoy the most about making beads?" Devin asked her.

"I like making the beads at home rather than working for a dollar a day in a quarry, crushing rocks with a hammer in the hot sun," she replied. "I am now making four to five dollars a day making and selling jewelry."

Even though I had seen slums in many places in the world, I suddenly felt nauseated and took a few steps backward, almost bumping into the wall. I felt embarrassed and ashamed as I thought of the comforts we had in the United States. This was a stark reminder of the poverty and of the precarious health status of millions of Africans. I felt deeply grateful to Devin and her team for their dedication and service to these women.

On safari in beautiful Murchison Falls National Park, we marveled at the lusciousness of the countryside and the wonders of the wildlife. The moon was starting to rise in the star-studded skies. Tiny white lights were strung among the trees in the eating area at the Nile River camp where we were staying. It was a magical setting, and we felt at home there. David and I decided that night that we must return to Uganda and put our clinical skills to good use by working in a hospital setting.

Kenya and Tanzania had captured my heart on visits there, but Uganda was special for its variety of terrain and warm, welcoming people. For years, David and I had talked about working together overseas in a health care setting while we still had the energy and health to make a difference. Given my international experience and David's skills as a medical doctor, his experience in the Peace Corps in Nigeria, and his work briefly at a hospital in Kenya, we decided to research hospitals in Uganda once back in the United States.

We had read that Africa has 6 percent of the world's population, 23 percent of the world's burden of disease, 66 percent of the world's AIDS cases, and only 3 percent of the world's health care providers. One of the hospitals, located in a remote part of Uganda, invited us to come the following spring.

We arrived in April the next year and stayed for a month, doing whatever we could to work together with the hospital staff. David and I returned for a month each year since 2005, bringing our medical students with us for a six-week internship project for a course we teach at the University of Colorado medical school. In 2006, we cofounded a nonprofit hospital project called the Uganda Malaria Health Care Project.

Shortly after our arrival that first spring, while walking along the dirt road that ran through the middle of the hospital campus, I was abruptly stopped by a young African man, running and waving his arms. "Make way for the ambulance!" he shouted. I looked for the ambulance and noticed what must have been serving as one. Two middle-aged men dressed in ragged blue jeans and T-shirts were carrying a makeshift stretcher with a sick young women lying on an orange blanket stretched between two thin, six-foot tree limbs.

Most people treated at this 250-bed hospital are peasant farmers living in mud houses with no electricity or running water. There is no town, except Mbarara, which is over eighty miles away. We were out in the middle of nowhere. There were no bright lights, no restaurants or paved roads—just people who lived in little shacks scattered around the surrounding area.

The hospital campus consisted of staff housing, nursing school housing, and a few buildings for seeing patients. There is a small administration building, a small., primitive operating room, and a chapel. The area has a high mortality rate from malaria, AIDS, and tuberculosis. The hospital is fifty miles from the Rwanda and Congo borders and able to exist because of hydroelectric power from a one-hundred-foot-tall waterfall in these highlands, which are about 4,500 feet above sea level.

That first night, we were given a small, cozy cottage with a small bed. We listened to the sounds of loud insects while in bed under our mosquito net. Our bodies were sore from the ten-hour car drive from Kampala over very rough roads.

It was hard not to be depressed by all the poverty; but from the minute I set foot on the hospital grounds, I felt warmth and was very aware of the urgent need of the people. They did not need immediate care from genocide and horrific trauma as much as simply a way to survive poverty and illness. I was learning that I couldn't accomplish anything good from a place of desperation, but only from a place of unconditional love for others and myself. This was humbling.

Working in Uganda brought me to a whole new level of understanding what it takes to be truly human. When I did field work in Kosovo, Syria, and the Israel/Palestine cultures, it opened up my sense of compassion for others' suffering. In Uganda, I knew I had to let go—again—of trying to "save" people or humanity and to just be present and use my skills.

A few days after arriving at the hospital, an eighteen-year-old nursing student named Eliza approached our little cottage on her way to get some fresh eggs from our neighbor's chickens.

"*Agandi*," I said, smiling.

She shyly replied in halting English, "I heard you speak in chapel about stress and trauma. Will you teach us how to help ourselves and then others?"

"Yes," I replied, remembering that the health care providers there did not openly talk about personal stress and emotional trauma.

"Where did you grow up? How did you get to nursing school here?" I asked. Over the next hour she told me through tears that her family had lost everything when the LRA (Lord's Resistance Army) burned their home. Their family of eighteen children had lost everything. Two of her older brothers were kidnapped by the LRA to become child soldiers, and she witnessed her mother's murder. She, her father, and some siblings escaped, but her father died of AIDS.

Eliza was grateful for receiving a nursing scholarship from the orphanage that had become her home, but she suffered from recurrent nightmares of her mother's death, and it was hard to study. "Can you help me?" she asked.

"You are experiencing PTSD, post-traumatic stress disorder," I replied. "I would be glad to help you."

This was a common story at the hospital. Traumatic stress and emotional and physical trauma were daily experiences, and the staff members were ashamed to share it with anyone. I was often approached in secrecy.

A few days later, Eliza told me that after our work with using somatic experiencing and EMDR, which are trauma therapy methods, her nightmares and headaches stopped for the first time since she was a child. She felt less guarded and happier, and it was easier for her to begin to forgive the LRA and to forgive herself for surviving.

What I learned from Eliza is that when I did not focus on all the suffering, I could let go of any sense of desperation I might have about her condition. Then I could truly help her.

I heard story after story from doctors, nurses, and teachers at the elementary school about their stress-related symptoms: ongoing headaches, stomachaches, and depression from working with very few supplies and lack of funding, and long work hours. I taught stress-management skills and the physiology of stress to the staff and nursing school, and David worked on the wards and did medical rounds. We learned that in the fifty years that the hospital had been open, the staff had never been supplied with Internet service or even mosquito nets.

One day, I climbed a small hill and sat down in the dirt, looking over the hospital campus below. I could see the rundown buildings between tall green trees. My chest tightened, and my breathing became labored. I felt sad and depressed because of all the poverty in that part of the world. *How can I help such overwhelming stress and suffering?* I asked myself. *Poverty and injustice is maintained through a government that does not promote equality for everyone.*

Taking a deep breath and coming to stillness and silence, I felt the soothing energy of oneness and unity flow through my body and all around me. I began to feel awe and gratitude once more, knowing that no matter how it looks, none of us is separate, and we are all being held in God's safety and love.

I heard insects buzzing and birds calling, and I saw beauty all around me. The Divine's presence was palpable in the potatoes growing on the hillside, the people walking the dirt road, the buildings that held the suffering patients, and the doctors, nurses, and others working so hard. When I reached for what is true in all of us and experienced that all-embracing tenderness, I felt the way love carries us all.

I went back to that hill many times on our trips to the hospital to restore myself. We all can heal through quieting our mind, being aware of the presence of the Divine, and trusting.

On one visit, Ellen, an American woman who was working in Uganda, contacted me when I arrived in Kampala. She had been working up north in the Gulu area with child soldiers who had been traumatized in their forced participation in the LRA and through Joseph Kony's horrible enslavement. Kony was the cult "Christian" prophet who captured and enslaved over twenty thousand children, mostly under the age of thirteen, to be his foot soldiers. He also killed and tortured children who tried to escape. *Where else in the world have there been twenty thousand kidnapped children?* I wondered.

The LRA and the bloody war between rebels and the Ugandan army had caused 1.6 million people to flee their homes and become refugees in their own country.

President Museveni's suppression of the Acholi tribal people in three northern districts of Uganda is generally believed to be the beginning of the LRA rebellion. The Acholi blame Museveni for the terror his forces committed and for denying the Acholi what they claimed was their share of international development funds. Kony formed the LRA army in his effort to overthrow Museveni. In the past twenty years, thousands of people have been killed in the conflict. Over these years, about fifteen thousand of the abducted children have been able to escape or have been rescued by Ugandan army forces.

Ellen had been working with one of the rehabilitation centers working to help restore the children's mental health. She offered me a chance to observe some of those who escaped and to witness one of the forgiveness ceremonies that the Acholi people offer to children who had been trained by Kony to kill their own family members as well as others. At the ceremony, I witnessed the African concept of *ubuntu*, which is respect for and appreciation of another's worth in a very deep way, mainly through forgiveness.

We arrived at an old warehouse building with paint peeling off the walls. Inside was one long room with folding chairs set up near the middle. I was able to talk to a skinny teenage boy named Matthew before we went through the forgiveness ceremony. He seemed much older than his age. He was wearing blue jeans and a Red Sox baseball shirt that was most likely donated by a Christian charity.

"Can you tell me something about your experience in the LRA," I asked.

Looking down at the floor, he quietly replied, "I felt terror the whole time. We had to walk miles and miles, always moving camp. If six- to eight-year-old boys complained of being tired, I was ordered to kill them."

"Did you kill them?" I asked, feeling my stomach cramp.

"Yes," he said, as his deep-brown eyes darted from side to side. It seemed to me that it was hard for him to focus.

"Also, I watched the men cut off a man's feet because he was riding a bicycle, and the rebels told me that the man was warning the Ugandan army where they were located. But the worst was when we came upon my family's hut, and I was forced to kill my father."

"How old were you when this happened?" I asked.

"Twelve years old," he replied with tears in his eyes.

The ceremony was about to start, and I thanked him with a long hug. I walked away in shock, my heart pounding and tears streaming down my cheeks.

The ceremony began with the boy standing on one side of a long, thick rope and his remaining family members standing on the other side, dressed in colorful dresses and shirts. Several young children sat on the floor. The Christian rehabilitation members, Ellen, and I were sitting on chairs behind Matthew.

The boy was asked by his uncle, his father's brother, to state his crimes against his family. The boy replied, "One night, I was forced by the LRA in a surprise attack on my family's home to kill my father, because they said he was a traitor to his tribal people. I shot him, and I am very sorry," he said with his voice cracking.

The uncle turned and looked at the family members and asked if they wanted to forgive this child because he was forced to do this crime.

"Yes," they all replied in loud voices.

The uncle looked at the boy and said, "You may cross over the rope now. Once you do, we will not mention this crime again. You are completely forgiven."

The boy stepped over the line, and the entire family surrounded him with hugs and smiles.

I cried through the entire ceremony, thinking, *How could humanity be this horrible to children? That family has to be very strong to forgive in that way. In our Western world, it seems much harder to forgive.* This was their child. They knew how crucial forgiveness was to his healing and to theirs. They were seeing the whole story, including the boy's trauma, with compassion.

The staff told us that this ceremony got results, and children who were forced to kill were once again loved and integrated back into their families. *But just how long does it last? They need to work on self-forgiveness as well,* I thought, as we left the building. Health care workers do come in and work with some of the children's emotional trauma, but so many are left without this important care.

Upon return to the States after our first visit to Kisiizi, we raised ten thousand dollars for the purchase and installation of a satellite dish because the hospital was so isolated and had no telephone communication with the outside world. In their valley, cell phones worked only sporadically. We continue to raise funds to support the maintenance of the satellite dish and bandwidth so that the staff could access up-to-date research and medical information. We also raised the money needed to provide mosquito nets for the entire staff and hospital wards.

My time in Uganda continues to affect me very deeply. So many areas of Africa suffer complications from poverty. It is hard not to be depressed about their circumstances. Yet the natural kindness and sense of community among the people—no matter how poor— opened my heart wider to the ongoing journey of finding ways to heal. Forgiveness of self and others is essential.

The amount of infectious disease, stress-related disorders, and emotional trauma among the people was overwhelming. At the same time, their love, acceptance, and wisdom shone through. The patients at the hospital did not want to be rescued; they wanted what we all want: health, healing, and employment to keep their families well.

Chapter 12

A Healing in Nature

Deep silence is an inner temple that allows for healing.

I dropped my backpack with three gallons of water and a sleeping bag as exhaustion took over, and I sank to the hard ground of reddish earth. It was a tiny area of rocks, stones, sagebrush, and juniper that I would call home for three solitary days and nights. The warm sun was shining brightly as I inhaled the smell of juniper. Looking around at the magnificent, unspoiled beauty of Southwest Utah, I suddenly wondered if there were any mountain lions or snakes living nearby. Cautiously looking around for places they might hide, I told myself, *Nothing to fear except fear itself.*

What am I doing? I asked, remembering our drive out of Boulder as we headed west to Moab, Utah, for our six-day vision quest. Stress from my daily responsibilities was left behind me. David was driving, and I sat in the passenger seat and stared out the window. We had signed up for the vision quest to go into the wilderness to replenish body and mind from our latest work overseas in Uganda.

I thought I knew what I was doing when I agreed to go. There alone, I thought, *Not so much now that I am in the wilderness without any protection from the elements and wild animals. Yikes!*

Sitting on the earth, looking around at the red rock mesas and majestic mountains in the distance, I could feel myself opening up to an inner soothing peace. The beauty of the natural world and the mountains grounded me. Gratefulness came alive deep within me, and I felt one with the natural world. I looked forward to the next three days of being alone. Being far away from anyone with only a sleeping bag and water was still questionable, however. *Stay in the moment*, I told myself, *and all will be fine.* Then I wondered, *How do we live peacefully in our own contradictions? Will this help my own healing, or will it be too hard?*

Elias and Rabia, our leaders, were staying at the base camp. They knew only our approximate location, and it felt like they were really far away. David and I started out to find our spots together but split up shortly after, so we were on our own quests.

I heard ravens cawing and allowed them to awaken my senses. Then I walked around the area I called home and gathered rocks and stones of all sizes. I made a circle around my sleeping bag and water bottles, praying over each stone: *This is my beloved home for three days. I pray for this precious part of earth to protect me from harsh weather or danger of any kind. Please open me deeper to my own divinity—my own true nature. Allow me to see and recognize what old beliefs do not work anymore, and help me to release them.*

Finishing my ritual, I felt much better. (I have turned to prayer since I was a small child.) I fell asleep during the heat of the afternoon and then woke up suddenly, hungry and disoriented. Fasting is supposed to empty the body and feed the soul. *Water—I must drink water.*

Streaks of red, pink, and orange lit up the nearby canyon as the sun dropped beyond the horizon, and it quickly became night. It was quiet. I watched as stars appeared one by one, and I snuggled into my sleeping bag. But sleep was elusive. I felt small and lonely. I allowed this loneliness to fill my being. *Why do I feel so lonely? It's only been a day so far. I love solitude. What is going on with me?*

I focused on the glimmering stars—hundreds of them. I felt how I was part of them—part of everything. Suddenly I heard growling nearby. My heart started to pound rapidly. I tried to slow down my breathing. *Is it a mountain lion?* I had no tent and was totally vulnerable. Then I heard the growl again, and I started laughing.

It was my stomach! I was totally relieved and dropped off to sleep shortly after that.

Sleepily I opened my eyes and watched the morning sun softly filter its way through the trees. Feeling empty, yet more spacious, I stayed cuddled in my sleeping bag for what felt like a long time. *What am I really here for? I am pushing fifty-nine years old. Fifty-something is manageable—but sixty?* I was afraid that my body without food for three days would not be able to walk me back to the base camp.

Fasting alone in the wilderness is an ancient, sacred rite of passage, I told myself. *Millions of people have done this at all ages. Can I experience aging with grace? Will this experience help me? Maybe. In this moment, the greatest gift I can give myself is to allow myself to be with the questions without needing answers. The answers will show up as I move through life.*

I decided to do an inquiry exercise that the founder of Radiant Mind, Peter Fenner, suggested we do. I started with asking the question "Who am I?" *Well, I know what I experience. But who is this "I" that knows what I experience? I can't see it, but I know that this awareness/consciousness is me—not my mind, but the intelligence that never changes and is always present. Not separate from anything. Everyone on the planet is aware. We just think we are separate.*

As I rested for a moment, I felt the soothing energy that comes from not thinking anything. *It is so much easier to do this exercise in nature—no distractions.*

One moment I was feeling empty and weary from thinking about the daily workings of life that past year, and the next I felt elated, feeling whole and complete in the beautiful wilderness and resting my soul. Later in the day, I felt unending joy with silence and grace all around. Everything was quiet. I could hear myself breathe even when I was moving around.

I thought about my years as a field biologist in my twenties, when I had spent days watching the behavior of Colorado birds in their natural habitat. I missed my deep connection with nature and the kind of work done in all kinds of weather. These days I was definitely a fair-weather biologist. No long, icy, cold days banding dippers that lived along Boulder Creek. There I was, soaking up the splendor of valleys, rugged canyons, and soaring mountains, releasing long-held stress points in my body and mind. I was unwinding from all bodily tensions and truly relaxing.

I thought of the psychology conference I had been to recently and a speaker who was talking about nature deficit disorder. *What would happen,* I thought, *if part of everyone's working day in the United States were spent in nature? Would illness decrease? Would people feel happier, less depressed? Mindfulness skills at work and their positive effects are well documented. What if walking every day in a natural setting and spending time in the wilderness once a year were mandatory?*

As I lay on my stomach on a warm, smooth rock, a small gray lizard and I watched each other. The lizard was close and sort of cute, and it could stay very still for a long time—longer than I could. When I moved first, it scampered away into a craggy crevice.

I turned over on my back and watched white, puffy clouds move slowly, softly in the clear blue sky. *The sky is endless, like consciousness,* I thought. I loved feeling the warm energy of ancient rock on my entire body.

Feeling expansive, I prayed for peace in the world and an end to conflict and poverty. I felt blessed that I could at least pray. I remembered my first real experience that the world wasn't just what science taught us. About thirty minutes after I had delivered Ryan in a natural birth and cradling that precious miracle in my arms, I could not believe how much love I felt for him. Love flooded my body and soul. Light filled the room, the drab green walls dissolved, and Ryan and I dissolved too. Feeling a deep sense of peace, I was not afraid—just amazed at the experience. All was soft light.

Divine grace was giving me a taste of serenity that seemed real yet otherworldly at the same time. I felt whole and part of that light. That holy moment of peace was the first step toward a new way of being in the world, as a mother and a seeker of spiritual consciousness, and my eventual change in career from a biologist to a psychotherapist.

My reverie continued into the afternoon. I pictured thirty-two years before, as my friend Jan and I walked our babies in strollers down our Boulder neighborhood street on a crisp autumn day. "You have got to experience this weekend seminar in Denver, called EST," she had said.

"I've heard that people are shouted at and are not allowed to go to the bathroom," I said.

Jan replied, "Oh, that is nonsense. It will change your life."

"Well, I do have this two-month-old baby to nurse day and night," I said.

"The EST training is a big part of the human potential movement that you are so interested in," she replied excitedly. "I will come with you and take care of Ryan at the hotel while you attend the seminar. I will bring him down to the seminar room so you can nurse him at breaks and lunch and any other times needed."

I stopped pushing the stroller and looked at her, stunned that she would do such a kind and enormous job for me, given she would have to take care of her own baby as well. I knew in that moment that it was meant to be.

And Jan was right. The experience I went on to have at the seminar changed my life. Sitting in the hotel ballroom for four days, I marveled at the competence of the trainers and what I was learning about human nature and myself. It was true: they yelled at some of us, keeping us out of our comfort zones. By not allowing us to go on bathroom breaks, they forced us to focus on a new way of thinking with no distractions. When Jan brought Ryan to the door, I would sit in the back of the room and nurse him as the training went on.

The trainers would occasionally come to the back of the room to look at Ryan and just melt with love for him. I was able to see right through the seeming harshness that was being played out in the training.

Late in the evening on the last day, we participated in an exercise that led us to experience our true essence or consciousness by finally letting go of our minds, our emotions, and our bodies. I experienced it for just a few moments. At first I was horrified. *Where am I?* I had disappeared—dissolved—with no ego to tell me I was a person with a personality. There was only the experience of nothingness and a sense that in that space I was not just a small separate self, but a vast, spacious Self.

I started laughing, sensing how much we take ourselves so seriously and that the reality of the spiritual world, where all is peace and love, happens at the same time as the physical world. The sense that my identity was no longer that of a separate self, but a part of all of life, all consciousness, and that everyone must be one with God was life altering. It's hard to explain that awareness, but I knew something had permanently shifted in me.

Eastern spirituality has taught about this vast Self for thousands of years, and I had the blessing of experiencing it for a few moments. I got intellectually that life is perfect as it is. In any moment, it does not have to change or be different. I understood that it is about who we are—not what we do or have or don't have. And most importantly, we are not just our bodies, emotions, thoughts, or achievements. We are not our stories, our wins, our losses.

I experienced other transformative changes after that seminar as well. The sinus headaches that I had experienced through my twenties stopped completely. My mind started to quiet down, and I no longer felt like I was a victim of life. I noticed how I had pretended to be someone I wasn't. I was afraid that if people knew that I thought or did things I was not proud of, they wouldn't like me.

Realizing that most of us do this made it easier to tell the truth about myself. My previous way of knowing was turned upside down. God was no longer a location in time and space, no longer outside of me, but a benevolent consciousness or awareness encompassing everything.

Back from my reverie, I was still in Utah, gazing at the clouds on my vision quest.

The third day, I wandered around the arid land, exploring new areas, hoping I would find my way back to my home base the next morning. I concentrated on every detail I could see: little flowers; smooth, warm rock; a small brown rabbit eating shrubs; the length of the canyon below and its winding valley.

Getting into my sleeping bag, I noticed that I wasn't hungry anymore. That was fascinating to me. At home, I often felt hungry—even when I had just eaten. The warmth and cozy feeling of my sleeping bag when the shadow of the pinion pine trees fell over it was comforting. I was almost through the third day. Silence became comforting as well—like something taking over my body and mind and allowing peace in a new way. I had nothing to do, nowhere to go.

The fourth morning, I awoke with a smile on my face. I was going to pack up and go back to base camp. It was a cloudy morning with a hazy glow of light. Packing up, I realized I had experienced a spiritual journey, not some heroic feat. As I stumbled back to the base camp with my backpack on, I realized how weak I felt because of not eating for three days. *How far is it?* I wondered. *What if I can't make it?* Finally I saw Rabia and Elias and heard them cheering me on with great enthusiasm. I actually felt a bit heroic. *Wow! I made it.*

Sitting at base camp, in a circle, we all shared some of what we had experienced and learned from our vision quests. I shared that I felt I could open myself up more to the deep pain in the world again, especially for work in Uganda, and not get buried in my own grief and despair. I felt more grounded in my love for life and the world, and stronger and clearer about the service work David and I were doing with our Uganda project.

I felt renewed resolve for recycling, for using less water and heat, for sustaining and deepening my relationship with family and friends, and for resting more and taking care of myself in a more tender way.

Apart from those highlights, listening to the deep silence for three days and nights was the most moving part of the vision quest for me. I did not necessarily come away with startling visions, but the deepening of my own relationship with myself was profound. It had been good to put myself in a place where I could let my mind stop for a while, to be silent inside and out.

We think that we have to be doing something always, so we don't let our minds and bodies rest. I settled into being more comfortable with myself, just the way I am, leaning into a power of healing that was given to me by being in and with nature.

Chapter 13

Miracle of Divine Consciousness

Healing comes from intentionality, inner calm,
and learning to live with uncertainty.

Our son, Ryan, came bounding into our home in June of 2007, waving a DVD that he had just rented at a local store. "Dad, Mom," he said excitedly, "you have to come downstairs and watch this new TV series. It will help you both to relax."

David and I were weary and distracted. A week earlier, David had returned home after an appointment with a neurologist and stated that he had just been diagnosed with Parkinson's, a medical condition without a cure. We were still feeling stunned, confused, and scared. "Dr. Dave" had always been the picture of health, and he worked at it too. He had exercised almost every day, eaten mostly healthy food, and taught good health practices to his thousands of family-practice patients over our twenty-seven years of marriage.

Knowing how deeply affected Ryan had been by his dad's new condition, I knew he wanted to help. We took popcorn downstairs, settled in on the couch, and waited to be entertained and to allow ourselves to let go of all stress. The popular series *Grey's Anatomy* started to play; it was about doctors and patients in a hospital setting.

The story was about a patient whose daughter was about to be married. The daughter told the doctors that she wanted her father to be healed after a planned surgery to be able to walk her down the aisle at her wedding. *What is wrong with the father?* I wondered. *Why can't he walk down the aisle with his daughter? Maybe it's a problem with a leg.*

The camera then zoomed in on the dad walking haltingly down the hospital hallway. He seemed stiff: his legs and arms were shaking, and they flew out at awkward angles. He could barely walk. He had Parkinson's.

I looked over at David. He was not breathing, staring straight ahead at the TV. Then I looked at Ryan. His face was ashen. I took a deep breath and started to laugh uncontrollably. This broke the tension, and Ryan and David joined in.

"Great, Ryan," I joked. "You sure brought over a program that would relax us!"

The universe has a crazy sense of humor. We watched the show until the end. The dad had deep brain stimulation surgery and was able to walk his daughter down the wedding aisle without shaking.

David had come home with his diagnosis the same week our annual ISSSEEM (International Society of Subtle Energy and Energy Medicine) conference was being held in Boulder. The keynote speakers and other presenters came to our home for the speaker's dinner.

"I heard about your situation, David," said an internationally well known healer. "I would love to give you a session." A medical doctor said compassionately, "David, I will send you a list of supplements that are well known for stabilizing Parkinson's." Another offered visualization work for healing. That he was diagnosed the week of the conference was holy synchronicity coming from God. I started to experience a sense of spaciousness, peace, and hope.

The following week, my friends Lila and Margo organized a healing prayer circle for David and me with Ryan and many of our closest friends. Love and support surrounded us, with each person letting us know how they supported us. When it came to Ryan's turn, he told everyone there, "I had a lot of anxiety over Dad's diagnosis and what it will entail for both him and my mom, but as I hear you speak, I feel so relieved and grateful to all of you." Community support is at the top of the list for healing.

The month that followed was an emotional roller coaster. We wanted to handle the devastating news with as much grace and equanimity as we could. My knowledge of different modes of healing was a blessing. I didn't feel helpless, knowing David and I had some skillful means to help us both. For three years, we had been enrolled in an ongoing course of study called Radiant Mind, taught by an Australian psychologist, Peter Fenner. A few weeks later, we met him for a long weekend in Boulder.

The first day, during meditation, I was aware of how much I had been trying not to suffer over David's prognosis for the future—that is, "a slow, neurological decline, with many different parts of his body not working well, needing full-time care at the end." *How will I handle being with the losses David will experience?* I thought. *Will I have the peace and understanding that's needed, or will I fold up in a ball and be a bundle of anxiety?*

After a while, I could drop into what Peter calls unconditional awareness—a soothing peace where no thoughts are present for a few minutes. I had experienced this as God's presence in the past, divine light that held everything, and light that surrounded and penetrated us. I could let any emotions or thoughts just be there and also experience them without judging or trying to get rid of them.

Later Peter asked to see to David and me privately. He could see that we were still carrying fear. He said, "When you are resting in unconditional or full awareness, the energy that is always present and never changes is a miracle. This unconditional awareness heals you, because it penetrates and dissolves the basis of all illness—namely, the story that we tell ourselves: that we are ill."

Something shifted for me in an instant. I felt a golden light traveling up my whole body, filling my mind and heart with pure goodness. This was much like the recurrent experiences in my childhood. I knew I could trust in this all-encompassing, unconditional intelligence, in God's presence, which resides in all of us. I thought, *Thank God for Peter Fenner being in our lives right now. I know we can handle this new challenge.*

With practice, it became easier to sink into this soothing energy, which is available to everyone. It shifted me from anxiety to peace. I began to notice the triggers preventing me from experiencing that state. I noticed that whenever that peace settled over me, I suffered less.

We continued seeing patients at our Colorado clinic and continued going to Uganda to do our volunteer work a month each year, often taking our medical students with us. We had to be very careful about the risk of infection for David, with infectious diseases being so prevalent at the Ugandan hospital.

And our story changed. We became a couple more deeply loving of each other; we transcended obstacles that would arise and that before would have thrown us off track. I felt the calming of my nervous system, as I was not trying to argue with reality so much. Most of the time it was fine if it was snowing; it was fine for the light of day to shorten in the winter; and—this had been a hard one for me—it was fine to let things be exactly as they were. We also noticed when we reverted to old patterns of trying to control outcomes instead of letting go.

When I would have an inevitable meltdown over a lack of control in even a trivial situation, a friend from my Boulder community was always there to remind me of how to dance in the paradoxes of life. I didn't have to have a problem with having a problem! Watching David be courageous through the following years was heart wrenching but also inspiring.

Challenges continued to come. We became more resilient on the one hand and more exhausted on the other. I felt so grateful for all the years I had put into learning about different ways of healing from all over the world. David was diagnosed with prostate cancer, and we began to use more ways of healing.

After researching all the data and interviewing different doctors, we decided to do "watchful waiting," which required checking in often with his main doctor for PSA tests. We continued to try alternative ways of healing. We came back to what we knew would help: eating well, acupuncture, exercise, tai chi, massage, visualization, and resting in unconditional awareness and God's presence as often as possible. Despite all this, David was told after three years that he would need prostate surgery.

In April 2011, we took a journey down to central Brazil to see the world-renowned healer John of God. I had expected more jungle-like vegetation, but we saw gentle green hills and occasional cows as we approached the small town of Abadiania. Many shops catering to tourists sold health food, clothing, and gemstones. Our guide on the bus mentioned that none of the shops sold pork, hot peppers, or alcohol, due to John of God's restrictions for the healing process. A pleasant floral fragrance greeted us as we arrived at our modest hotel, but David could not smell well due to the Parkinson's.

A month earlier, our dear friend Roger had called and told us that he and his wife were going down to see John of God for two weeks. He wanted us to join him. We were deeply grateful for the scholarship we received for the cost of the trip and for the way Roger was able to arrange our flights and passports at the last minute.

David and I, sitting motionless with eyes closed, were saying silent prayers in the meditation, or "current," room a few feet away from John of God. Christian music was playing softly in the background, helping us to concentrate deeply on God's holy presence. I felt intense energy all around us as twelve prearranged meditators in this area of the L-shaped room were deep in prayer. I smelled the strong scent of roses, which kept me from being tempted to open my eyes.

One by one, pilgrims from all over the world, dressed in white, moved forward in a line and presented their specific requests for healing to this humble trance healer. John of God is a vessel for healing energies that come through him, and he is not aware afterward of what happened.

David and I were suddenly shaken gently by one of John of

God's assistants. She said quietly, "John of God wants you both to come forward and sit on chairs directly in front of him."

We walked over to the chairs and sat down quietly. John of God, with graying hair, dressed in his usual white shirt and pants, guided a woman dressed in white pants and blouse to stand next to him.

The assistant brought over a tray with several small, sharp knives on it and placed it on a table next to John of God. The assistant translated from Portuguese for us as John of God said, "This woman flew here from Germany yesterday. She has an extreme health situation consisting of a hernia on her left side. She has had no anesthetic or pain pills. We will do surgery now."

The chosen meditators behind us and at an angle tried to see what was happening. They were supposed to have their eyes closed, but since this was so out of the ordinary, everyone was watching.

John of God took a knife from the tray, raised the women's blouse up a bit, and made a deep cut into her side below the rib cage. Bright-red blood flowed out onto her white pants and all over the floor by our feet. She did not flinch or move, as if she felt nothing. I felt disoriented and a bit dizzy.

John of God said something to his assistant. She told David that John of God was asking for him to stand up and assist him with the surgery. We did not know how he knew David was a doctor. He asked David to feel into the women's wound. David felt into the wound with his hand and withdrew it, blood dripping from his fingers.

"Can you feel the hernia?" he asked. "Will you please tell the people in this room what you have experienced?"

David turned around to the onlookers and said, "I could not find any indication of an existing hernia. It appears that this women has been healed."

John of God's assistant gave him a needle and thread from the tray, and he stitched up the woman while she seemed to feel no pain. She was taken to the recovery room and would stay for twenty-four hours.

David sat down next to me, looking a bit shaken. An assistant wiped up the blood from the floor, and I asked her if David could have a towel to wipe the blood off his hands. We tried to process the miracle that had just happened.

We were told that millions of people from all over the world have received gifts of healing through this man, who never accepts payment for his work. For fifty years, he has stated, "I never healed anybody. It is God who heals."

We walked around the lush grounds of the Casa, as it is known, and could feel a loving energy in the earth and fragrant flowers and fruit trees. David was stunned when he could smell the strong fragrance. Each day, we sat in devotion on wood benches overlooking a lush valley below. We were told that John of God did not do physical surgery very often. Mostly, pilgrims are asked to sit in a room where spiritual/invisible healings are given by "angels of God" or "entities."

Sitting on a chair in the "spiritual surgery" room, I was stunned when I felt what seemed like invisible hands in my intestines. I instinctively felt that it was crucial for me to let go of a past emotional wound, to forgive others, and to live in the present. I had asked for healing of long-time intestinal distress since 1999 in Kosovo.

After spiritual surgery, we were required to stay in our sparse hotel rooms for twenty-four hours. Hotel assistants delivered food to our room. I felt very weak during that time, but once back home, I felt intestinal relief for the first time. David felt changed by his experience as well and had a stronger belief in spiritual healing.

We ran into the German woman before we left the Casa and asked her how she was feeling. "Great," she said. "I no longer feel the intense pain I had for months before coming here. Do you want to take a look at the surgery?" David gladly looked and could see that it was healing rapidly.

There are many different ways of healing, and what really heals is unconditional spiritual love. We felt this at the Casa, and we returned home deeply convinced. But we were crushed when David's x-rays showed that he would still need to have prostate surgery. He began the two-month radiation treatment. At first he continued to see patients, but he became exhausted and was forced to retire suddenly after thirty-three years of practicing family medicine at the medical center that we had cofounded.

I decided to retire from our medical center as well, and I moved my practice to a Boulder office. We both felt the sudden, deep loss of devoted care to three generations of patients in the Louisville/Lafayette area of Boulder County.

Grief and fear overwhelmed us. We loved our work and needed to work to provide for ourselves financially. For the previous few years, we had been studying with another remarkable teacher, Candice O'Denver, who was influencing thousands of people around the world with her education program called Balanced View. Her loving support and insight helped us to overcome our fear and many hurdles that were to come.

David was hired part time as the medical director of a large hospice, seeing patients and directing the staff. I continued to see patients in Boulder. During that time of sudden change, we were surprised and delighted to receive the United Nations International Human Rights Award for our humanitarian work over the years, both individually and together. We were also given a Congressional Certificate Award for our service to our community. This gave a great lift to our spirits.

I learned so much about healing over those years. Healing can be instantaneous, which has been a mystery to the medical field throughout history. Healing energy has been shown to flow through cells in our bodies and to create low-frequency electromagnetic fields around us. These energy flows seem to come back to normal through intention, prayer, and God's or universal energy.

Our own biochemistry and energy fields are thought to be inseparable from universal energy, or what some researchers call unconditional consciousness. This awareness is not conditioned in the moment by past experiences. Quantum physicists are working with more subtle forms of vibrational energy. Scientific research is showing amazing potential in self-regulatory techniques, self-healing, and the fields of epigenetics and neurogenesis.

John of God and other healers demonstrate that healing of any illness requires a lot more than psychopharmacology or medical surgery. Most of the time it takes intentionality, a calm state, and connection to the source of life on all levels: physical, mental, emotional, and spiritual.

Chapter 14

How to Resist Nothing

*Grace is always present, even if we don't
open our awareness to see it.*

I sat in a Denver hospital room, holding my beloved mother's frail, purple- veined hand, as she was dying of heart failure and pneumonia at the age of ninety-nine and a half. The night before she had rallied. "Mom," I asked her then, "are you aware that you will most likely go to rehab tomorrow?"

Mom had been through intense rehab three years earlier in Wisconsin after breaking her hip and month-long rehab for pneumonia the last two winters. "Yes," she said, "the doctors have told me that I need to go to rehab. I'm so tired, Chris, but glad you are here. How are you doing with your car accident injuries?" She fell asleep before I could answer, and I quietly left the hospital thinking, *She is so sick, but still she thinks lovingly of my well-being.*

Mom was a star rehab patient and was always released earlier than the doctors predicted. She worked hard, pushing her walker down the halls and using the equipment well. Everyone admired her positive attitude and sense of humor. Up until three years ago, she had been living alone but close to my older brother. She had lived a vital life. Every summer she swam laps in Lake Geneva and worked part time for the Avon Corporation until she was ninety-two.

Mom had been in rehab in Denver the year before, recovering from pneumonia. I knew she was tired and wasn't up to any more rehab work at almost one hundred years old. The next morning, the doctors told us she was actively dying. I resisted this fact all the way to the hospital. But, once there, I moved into a more accepting state. This was not easy.

My sister, Camille, and I were distressed over Mom's labored breathing, as were Ryan, and my niece, Megan. I asked if David could do anything about it. David left the room to ask Mom's doctors to ease her distress. Knowing his background as a hospice doctor for the past two years, they asked him to make adjustments.

He knew exactly what needed to be done. He adjusted her oxygen and morphine levels throughout the next seven hours, so Mom's breathing became easier, and our anxiety became less. I looked at David and said, "Why don't more hospital doctors know how to administer loving palliative care to ease dying patients' suffering?"

Goodie, as Mom was affectionately known, was probably one the most positive and loving people I have ever known. Yes, we had our differences along the way, as all mothers and daughters do, but we always tried to listen and understand. As I sat by her bed, holding her hand, I knew I would miss her delight in telling jokes to anyone and everyone, and then laughing right along with them.

When I was ten years old, wearing my new school clothes, I remember being in the kitchen with Mom, who was holding a cup of coffee. She told me that we live in a culture that worships false promises—like the belief that money and material gain bring lasting happiness. She said, "I hope you live your life with a decision to love and serve others. That will make you happy." That wisdom from her has sustained me my entire life.

Still at her bedside, Camille and I read passages from the Bible to Mom. Mom loved to sing, and she sang in her church choir until she was ninety-two. We decided to sing some of her favorite songs. We sang "An Apple Grows on a Lilac Tree," a song she sang to all her children, grandchildren, and great-grandchildren. I knew she could hear us, though her eyes were closed. The hand I was holding became more relaxed.

All of us rotated in and out by her bedside. There was plenty of time to think and to grieve. I thought I was prepared for it. I guess we are never prepared for the finality of a mother's death.

"Mom," I said to her, with tears streaming down my cheeks, "You have been so caring over all these years and a gift of wisdom to everyone. You will always be with me. You taught me so much, but three things stand out: to love God, to love others, and to be of service. I am so grateful for your guidance." I continued to speak words of love and appreciation to her throughout the day.

Mom was mentally sharp her entire life and had an incredible memory for the details of everyone's lives, even at the age of ninety-nine. We knew her death was coming, given her age, but it was not obvious. She did not suffer from major illnesses.

Camille and I, David and her two grandchildren, Ryan, and Megan, took turns holding her hands and stroking her forehead. Her forehead was so soft and smooth. David checked on Mom again and told us that she was just about ready to make her transition.

Camille came over to me and said, "I just can't bear to watch her last moments. Forgive me, but I have to leave." I understood how difficult Mom's dying process was for my sister. Her care of Mom the last three years was a wonderful gift, and at the same time, was a round-the-clock job. We had moved Mom from Lake Geneva to Denver to live with Camille three years before. David, Ryan, and I would drive to Denver as often as we could to give Camille a break and some time to herself. My two brothers and I had hired someone to be with Mom during the day, while Camille worked, but she was caring for Mom the rest of the time.

I could feel Mom's life force slipping away and then I heard her last breath. "Go with God, Mom," I whispered. *Dying is like living,* I thought. *You can't control it. But I want to control this. What will I do without her physically in my life? I feel so empty inside—like I can't breath.*

With tears in my eyes, I thanked God for hearing all our prayers for her peaceful crossing. I felt a wonderful, soft light and energy permeate the room. Just then my cell phone rang. It was my older brother, Craig. He had been with Mom at the hospital and had returned to his home in Wisconsin the night before. "Mom just took her last breath," I said, hardly able to speak.

"Chris," Craig said, "please take off Mom's wedding rings, and give them to Camille." This startled me, as Mom had already given away everything she owned to us. But I knew she had promised her wedding band to my daughter, Shannon, her engagement ring to me, and her other diamond ring to her granddaughter, Megan. Camille had said many years before that she did not want a ring.

"Really?" I asked Craig. "Mom promised those rings to Shannon and me."

"No," he said. "Mom wanted them to go to Camille." He then had to hang up. The phone rang again, and it was our younger daughter, Shannon. I told her Mom had just died and what my brother told me about the rings. She felt sad about Grandma dying and surprised and confused about the rings.

I removed Mom's rings from her precious hand and then climbed up on the bed and lay beside her. Gently kissing her, I said my final goodbye. I felt disoriented, and grief overwhelmed me.

On the way home, I called my sister about the rings and finally began to understand the last-minute change Mom had made. "A few days ago, Mom told me that she wanted me to have the rings because I had taken care of her and she had nothing else to give me," she said.

"I understand completely," I replied. "But what should we do about Shannon?"

The rings had been soldered together because Mom's hands had become so slender and delicate. We decided that we would separate the wedding band from the engagement ring and give the wedding band to Shannon and engagement ring to Camille. I went to bed that night feeling sad about Mom's passing and yet feeling better about the rings. I really wanted one of Mom's rings, because I felt it would help me with my grieving. Yet I had many precious things from her home that warmed my heart when using them to serve meals or just seeing them. I could feel my mother close to me as I finally drifted off to sleep.

The next morning, as I was getting dressed, I opened my wooden jewelry box. I was shocked by eleven two-inch vertical scratches on the inside of the lid, right above my rings. I knew the scratches had not been there the day before. And David would certainly not have done that. I was stunned. Taking a deep breath, I felt that Mom was trying to reach me about the rings.

I had heard about strange things like this happening around loved ones who have just died. And Mom never did like any kind of misunderstanding among her children. It made sense that she was trying to eliminate any disharmony. I wondered, *Is communication really going on from the other side?*

In the afternoon, Brenda, a good friend, stopped by our home to see how I was doing and to offer support. "Brenda, thank God you are here!" I said. "I have to show you something extraordinary." We went upstairs to the jewelry box, and Brenda was just as stunned as I was. However, she too knew of such happenings from other people's stories.

"What do you suppose the number eleven might mean?" she asked.

"I don't know," I replied. "Let's start counting the rings from the top clockwise." I was surprised when the eleventh ring turned out to be one I had forgotten about: my great-grandmother's ring from Norway.

I slid the tiny diamond ring on my little finger and have worn it every day. I had been given a ring from Mom after all. I'd like to think that my mother was letting me and my siblings know that her body had died, but her love was still guiding us. This was so healing for me, and I knew that healing comes in many different forms.

The first year after Mom's death was an emotional roller coaster. I just could not understand life without my mother in it. She had been with us for so long. During Mom's last year, we'd had many conversations about death and how she felt about it.

My dad had died twenty years before, and most of her friends and family were already gone. We talked about how your body and brain wear down, but how your spirit stays alive and well. At least *her* spirit did.

"Mom, how will you feel about letting your body go when it's time for your transition?" I had asked gently one warm sunny day as we sat outside on our patio. "Do you think you will feel calm and enfolded in God's eternal love?"

She looked at me for a minute and said, "You know, your dad used to quote Woody Allen all the time: 'I don't mind dying as long as I don't have to be there.' He thought that was funny."

"Yes," I said, "but we knew he was afraid of dying."

"Well, I feel differently about it. I know I will be in God's hands with nothing to fear, and I want to see my sisters and parents again." I felt her truth and admired her for it. She was not resisting the inevitable.

Over the last three years of her life, my mother continued to contribute to society. She would stand up at the front of the room, holding onto her walker, and give motivational pep talks to the homeless who came to my sister's Homeless Project in Denver. They loved her! She would always finish with one of the many of jokes she had memorized.

My mother loved to laugh, loved visiting with people, and loved to serve. She was grateful for everything she had. Her kindness to all was an inspiration. It was healing to be with her during her last days and truly a blessing to be with her during her last breath. I feel her soul's presence every day. I long for her every day, and then I tell myself, *Let it all be the way it is. Resist nothing.*

Epilogue

Living in harmony with the way things are is the hallmark of healing.

One morning this spring, I woke up feeling awe and great happiness as I recalled the dream I'd just had. It was what I call a *big* dream, because the wisdom gained is profound.

I remember every detail. I was at the Hotel Colorado, located in the Rocky Mountains, for a psychotherapy conference. One of my colleagues, Carol, was telling a small group of us about an old temple she had come across in her walk through a wooded area near the hotel. Even though our evening meeting was about to start, I decided to go to see the temple before it got dark.

As I walked where Carol had described, I finally found the temple. I looked around hesitantly, as it was almost dark, and no one else was around. I was nervous but decided to enter. It looked very old and sacred, with small, flowered altars on each side of the room lit with candles. Nearing one altar, I saw there was a hole the size of a large bush in the center. Peering inside, I saw a tunnel leading down to a small cave-like room where a soft light was shining.

I slid down the smooth surface of the tunnel, and the soft light changed to a brilliant one that filled the tiny room. I felt warm and safe as comforting arms embraced me. I felt myself being held and had no need to hold myself up. A deep peace settled over me, and I knew I had fallen into the arms of God.

This dream and all I have learned about living life with a sense of joy and aliveness have sustained me this past year. After my mother died, David contracted pneumonia that quickly moved beyond the pleural cavity. Surgery saved his life, and he made an amazing recovery. The way our three children helped to care for him while he was in intensive care for six days at the hospital was an enormous gift. Certainly that loving care helped David heal more quickly than anything else.

Devin, Ryan, Shannon, and I took turns staying with him around the clock that week, bringing him organic food and helping him to manage numerous tubes and machines. Our amazing and dearly loved son-in-law, Mark, stayed at our home with our two grandchildren and brought them to the hospital each day. David was surrounded by our love and his beloved family's support. Brad, who is like a son to us, and a circle of close friends were there when we needed them, providing food and other help. After two more weeks in rehab, David was home again in his own familiar surroundings.

Learning how to receive and give love is what nourishes our souls and heals us, even beyond any treatment or medicine. But for me, having faith in the unconditional divine consciousness that is everywhere is essential. I do believe that the true nature of the universe is woven out of the fabric of sacred love and goodness.

The more I live, the less I know. Life is constantly sending us change and mystery. But I do feel that I was given this life to learn that in our deepest nature, we basically want to love and be loved. But can we let ourselves be loved—not just by others but by the entire universe? By God? This isn't easy to do, because we judge ourselves and everything else.

I believe that everything—this entire universe—*is* love and that we can live *as* that love/unconditional awareness/Christ light, no matter how we each name that soothing energy. It's always present and never changes. That is a miracle and a mystery as well. We really can't describe this universal ground of conscious intelligence. Our own awareness is this universal ground.

All the experiences we have growing up and throughout our life shape us. But in the final analysis, we know that neurological systems are associated with resilience and healing. My baby boomer generation is getting older. In our twenties, we thought we could control our lives and bring about beneficial change. Now life seems to work better when we focus on things over which we have some control and let go of the things we can't control.

We experience our lives with joy as well as pain. Our lives can be a fast river taking us under, making it hard to breathe, or can carry us into the flow of peace and well-being. There is a compelling body of evidence that says the mind is not local and that it can affect and interact with other humans and all beings—without our conscious knowledge or awareness.

Post-traumatic stress has captured my attention and been part of my work over the past thirty years. But these days I also want to concentrate on a post-traumatic *growth* response for the whole field of healing. I heard somebody casually say this phrase at a conference and thought it was a great reframing—from distress to healing. There is an old saying in Zen Buddhism: "If you fall down on the ground, it is the ground you use to get yourself up again." Challenges really do become opportunities.

The world is beginning to wake us up to a new way of relating. It doesn't take dying to know that there is a divine presence that greets us with a profound love that we can hardly imagine. When we take the time to rest into this presence, whether it is through meditation, prayer, relaxation exercises, mindfulness, or holy moments in nature, we experience this unconditional love that has always been here and is steadfast.

Grace is always present, even if we don't open our awareness to it. Excessive thought, worry, media exposure, and fear can overwhelm us on a daily basis. Our conditioning throughout life seems to create a false sense of knowing the nature of who we really are and why we suffer so much. We are much more than just our personality. I believe that the fundamental ground of our being is spirit or divine consciousness.

I learned that it is possible to be engaged in the world where we feel all of it, but we do not have to change it just because we don't like it. Hope is indeed important. I love the definition of hope by the former president of the Czech Republic, Vaclav Havel: "Hope is an orientation of the heart and of the spirit. It is not the belief that things will work out well, but that things make sense, however they turn out."

I know from my own experience that when I don't argue with reality, my suffering is less. I feel healing taking place and feel more connected with people and nature. I have less judgment of others and myself, and forgiving others and myself becomes easier. I can find peace more often in each moment, no matter what terrible thing is happening. And, as we all know, many terrible things have been happening. At the same time, this does not mean that we shouldn't take action to better our conditions.

Listening more deeply to what people are saying—and for what is not being said—is paramount. I know I will make mistakes. I hope I will continue to learn from them. I find myself overwhelmed with gratitude and the grace of life itself. It has become much easier to understand other people's perspectives and beliefs, whether or not I adhere to those values myself. Fear arises in my body and mind, but I hope to move forward with trust that I am held in the greatest love we can possibly know.

The whole world seems to be igniting a flame in its heart. The power of people working together interculturally is taking hold. Modern physics has shown us that the entire world is an undivided wholeness. Even when I worked in countries that have enormous restriction on freedom, I felt this change taking place in individuals and families, and especially in women. And yes, war and human violence continue to escalate, and dread and despair enter our lives way too often through media.

By working with people's emotional trauma on many scales (including my own), I have learned the importance of taking risks and walking into the unknown. More and more, I find people taking action by following their hearts and listening to their innermost desires for the benefit of all.

What if we experienced a world where everyone felt welcomed, where each human being knew that he or she truly belongs? As Ryan said at the age of five, his ultimate wish was "to whisper into the ears of all people and say, 'You are not alone!'"

Acknowledgments

Writing this memoir involved a lot of support and encouragement. I am deeply grateful for the support, close company, and love from my friends, colleagues, and family. To name each person would require many pages. So I want to name a few who have especially influenced the stories I have written.

I am immeasurably grateful to my dear and loving friend and colleague, Joan Borysenko. Thank you for writing the beautiful foreword to this book and for giving me much-needed advice on the final draft. And thank you for all the joyous and challenging times we have shared over the past twenty-three years and for being available at all times with your incredible compassion and consistent, sisterly love.

To Gordon Dvierin, who graciously organized fun and relaxing road trips, dinners, and tremendous heart-felt caring for all of us over the past ten years. You continue to inspire me with your love of life and knowledge of just about everything.

A heartfelt thanks goes to Cinda Johnson, Wayne Muller, and Judy Schilling for giving me feedback on the first draft of the book. I am especially grateful to Judy for her excellent feedback on the final draft. Thank you to Suzanne Ewy, for her gift of proofreading, and thank you to Janet Stevens for help with the design of this book's cover.

And to Brad Machamer, Tom and Deborrah Willard, Jan Baulsir, Elena and David Johnston, Bobbi and Richie Dash, Margo King, John Steiner, Lalla and Rinaldo Brutoco, and Carol Schneider, for their loving friendship and nourishing care.

To my parents, Gudrun and George Curry, I give thanks for the gift of life, and I am especially grateful to my mother, who encouraged me to write and publish this book, even as she was in the process of dying at almost one hundred years old.

I am grateful for the leading-edge thinkers and teachers I have studied with, especially Dr. Robert Shaw, Father Thomas Keating, Dr. Jim Gordon, Dr. Carol Schneider, Rabbi Zalman Schacter-Shlomi, Dr. Peter Fenner, and Candice O'Denver. And I give a deep bow to Max Regan for his gracious encouragement to write this memoir, for his creative writing class, and for content development editing. Thank you to the team at Balboa Press, who guided me through the publication process.

Thanks to the staff at our hospital in Uganda and my international teammates on the Healing the Wounds of War Project in Kosovo, who made it possible for me to write many of the stories.

To the amazing and resilient refugees and survivors of war—you have taught me so much about the nature of being human.

To my children, Shannon, Ryan, and Devin Hibbard, and son-in-law, Mark Jordahl, thanks for all your support and love.

And finally, to my husband, colleague, and best friend, David Hibbard, for thirty-seven years of loving support, lessons learned, and patience. Your care and love during my writing process and recovery from my car accident was above and beyond the call to the deepest kind of service.

Resources

- *Association for Comprehensive Energy Psychology*

An organization for psychotherapy, coaching, and health care treatment that works with the mind-body connection for relief from trauma and stress.

http://www.energypsych.org

- *The Association for Global New Thought*

An organization for planetary healing through self-realization and spiritually motivated activism.

http://agnt.org

- *Balanced View*

A global grassroots movement focused on mental and emotional stability and life-satisfaction in order to inspire each person to use his or her strengths to benefit a greater good of all.

Candice O'Denver

http://www.balancedview.org/en/

- *Bead for Life*

An international organization that creates sustainable opportunities for women to lift their families out of extreme poverty by teaching them the skills and confidence they need to be entrepreneurs, to learn self-generated earning opportunities, and to have holistic support.

https://www.beadforlife.org

- *Boulder Integral Stress Management Clinic*

Dr. Christine Hibbard, PhD, provides leading-edge integral psychotherapy and education for mind-body-spirit health and human consciousness. The clinic treats individuals and couples in psychotherapy, biofeedback, and emotional trauma and other strategies for relieving stress.

www.christinehibbard.com

- *The Canfield Training Group*

Jack Canfield, an internationally recognized leader in peak performance strategies and the best-selling author of *The Success Principles* and the Chicken Soup for the Soul series, offers transformational trainings to individuals and organizations.

www.jackcanfield.com

- *The Center for Mind-Body Medicine*

An international organization for mind-body medicine that creates communities of healing by using strategies for relieving stress, transforming trauma, and promoting life-long health.

James Gordon, MD

http://cmbm.org

- *Haelan Lifestream Center*

The Haelan Lifestream Center offers tools for healing, evolution, and growth in the areas of body and spirit.

John Day, MD

http://drjohnday.com

- *Eye Movement Desensitization and Reprocessing International Association (EMDRIA)*

An international organization utilizing EMDR therapy and providing information to the greater EMDR community, clinicians, and researchers in order to promote the standards for EMDR to treat a variety of symptoms.

http://www.emdria.org

- *Foundation for Conscious Evolution*

An organization for evolving universal humanity and for connecting and co-creating.

Barbara Marx Hubbard

https://www.evolve.org

- *The Foundation for Living Medicine*

A foundation that focuses on health care based on individual's conscious choice and guidance for their "physician within" for life and healing.

Gladys McGarey, MD

http://www.thefoundationforlivingmedicine.org

- *Diane Poole Heller*

Diane presents trainings on somatic attachment and trauma.

http://www.dianepooleheller.com

- *Hollowdeck Press, LLC*

Max Regan is a developmental editor helping authors create and edit books. He is also the founder and director of Hollowdeck Press, LLC, offering creative-writing classes to groups nationally and internationally.

Max Regan, MFA

http://www.Hollowdeckpress.com

- *HOLOS University*

A university that aims to prepare students to integrate the universal principles of spirituality and holistic health through self-development, scholarly exploration, and compassionate service.

https://www.holosuniversity.org

- *Institute of the Southwest*

An educational organization dedicated to the liberation of wisdom, collaboration, wholeness, and transformative change.
Wayne Muller
http://www.waynemuller.com

- *International Society of Subtle Energies and Energy Medicine (ISSSEEM)*

An organization that aims to unify science and the spirit in order to encourage cooperation of subtle energies and that encourages scientific and intuitive exploration of integrative healing and applied spirituality.
http://www.issseem.org

- *Mind-Body Health Sciences, LLC*

Dr. Borysenko provides education about the intersection of the mind and body health, positive psychology, and spiritual exploration to better encourage a life of multidimensional caring for body, mind, and soul.
Joan Borynsenko, PhD
http://www.joanborysenko.com

- *National Parkinson's Foundation*

An organization whose mission is to help every person diagnosed with Parkinson's to live the best possible life through expert care and research. Their website provides information, blog posts, and videos.
http://www.parkinson.org

- *One Spirit Interfaith Seminary*

A seminary whose mission is to be an interspiritual institute that offers in-depth experiential education and professional training to teach, ordain, and prepare spiritual leaders, and to support and nurture an individual's spiritual development.
http://onespiritinterfaith.org

- *The Path of Ceremonial Arts*

A program that provides spiritual and ceremonial practice based on love of the Divine.

Lila Tresemer

http://thestarhouse.net/pca/

- *Path of the Friend*

An institute that works with spiritual teachers and citizen-diplomats who work for peace in areas of conflict around the world; they are focused primary in Asia and the Middle East.

Elizabeth Rabia Roberts, EdD

Pir Elias Armadon

http://pathofthefriend.org

- *Patient Family Physician Guide*

A medical directive written by Drs. Christine and David Hibbard for individuals to make choices for end-of-life care with their family's agreements.

Christine Hibbard, PhD

www.christinehibbard.com

- *Radiant Mind*

An organization that provides a structured course that uses Dr. Peter Fenner's training in Asian nondual wisdom to increase unconditioned awareness that can create liberation, egolessness, pure essence, and being.

Peter Fenner, PhD

http://www.radiantmind.net

- *Shealy Wellness*

A website that provides information on depression, stress management, and pain resolution from Dr. Norm Shealy, who specializes in resolution of chronic pain and is a leading expert in

pain and depression. The website allows for consults, talks, and events with Dr. Shealy.
Norman Shealy, MD
https://normshealy.com

- *Spiritual Directors International (SDI World)*
An inclusive global learning community that serves and supports ministry and service of spiritual direction.
http://www.sdiworld.org

- *Transformational Leadership Council*
A council that aims to bring together leaders of personal and organizational transformation together in order to support each other and their worldwide contributions.
http://www.transformationalleadershipcouncil.com

- *Uganda Malaria and Healthcare Project*
A nonprofit organization serving Kisiizi Hospital in Southwest Uganda, bringing health care values and funding to improve the level of health care in that region.
David Hibbard, MD
Christine Hibbard, PhD
http://ugandamalariahealthcareproject.weebly.com